CLIMBING YOUR INNER MOUNTAIN

Ten Steps to Reaching Any Goal

BY
ROBERT SHUMAKE

TAKE THE LAND PUBLISHING
DETROIT, MI

Climbing Your Inner Mountain: Ten Steps to Reaching Any Goal
Published by Take the Land Publishing
Detroit, MI

Copyright © 2013 by Robert S. Shumake

ISBN: 978-0-615-80360-9

Printed in the United States of America
First Edition May 2013

Cover Design by: Marlon E. Hines
Interior Design by: A Reader's Perspective
Editing and Proofreading by: Make Your Mark Editing Services

CLIMBING YOUR INNER MOUNTAIN

Ten Steps to Reaching Any Goal

100% of the proceeds for
Climbing Your Inner Mountain: Ten Steps to Reaching any Goal will go to the Shumake Family and Friends Foundation to help educate our youth.

Thank you for your contribution.

ACKNOWLEDGMENTS

Throughout this incredible journey—from the climb of Mount Kilimanjaro to the composition of *Climbing Your Inner Mountain*—I have been blessed to experience an insurmountable level of support and encouragement. Had it not been for the amazing people in my life, there to cheer me on, give insight, challenge me, believe in me, and just say, "You can do it" and sometimes, "You *can't* do it," I would not have a story to tell. Thank you all.

I must first give honor to God who, during my ascent of Mount Kilimanjaro, showed me who He *really* was. Had it not been for my unyielding faith in the Creator, I am certain that I would not have survived the journey to tell my story today. To my friend Tebebu Tsadik, thank you for agreeing to join me on this wild ride to the top of Africa's highest peak. Your presence there with me on that mountain gave me the added strength I needed and propelled me forward with each agonizing step to the finish. To Mama Ja' Phia, thank you for inspiring me to write and supporting everything I do.

To my key players, thank you for the talent, commitment, and diligence it took to bring this book to life: Janaya Black, the first person with whom I shared the idea, who helped me take the book from brain to ink, Anthony Neely, who forced me to tell my side of the story and share the real Robert Shumake with readers, Pam Perry, my social media whiz, Andrew Morrison of Small Business Camp, the consensus builder, who kept the team together, my publicity guru, Trea Davenport of Trea Day Management and Publicity, and Monique D. Mensah of Make Your Mark Editing, my proofreader extraordinaire, consultant, and go-to person for everything from e-books to self-publishing.

To my children, Jamelia, Diop, and Amina, my sisters and brother, Nikita, Nehru, and Norflette, my father, Robert Shumake Sr., who taught me to think positive, and the rest of my wonderful family, thank you for inspiring me to follow my dreams and tell my story.

Thank you, Darren Coleman, Adrienne Lance Lucas, and Keno Lucas II and the Keno Foundation for all of your support. To the coaches, officials, and students, thank you for helping to make the Shumake Relays so great. I would also like to acknowledge Ambassador Neil Parsan of Trinidad and Tobago, Ambassador Tebelelo Seretse of Botswana, and Suleiman Saleh of the Tanzania Embassy. A big thank you to the people who prepared me for the climb: the team from Backcountry North for outfitting me, my meditation coach, Delrico, my breathing coaches, Amin, Sarah, and Jahki, and my trainers, Darian and Dave.

For anyone that I may have forgotten to mention, please blame the omission on my memory and not my heart, and remind me to thank you in person.

This book is dedicated to Steve Myen, who taught me that our greatest mountains are discovered within. If we are able to climb or conquer ourselves then greatness in the world is certain.

TABLE OF CONTENTS

AUTHOR'S NOTE

"So be sure when you step, step with care and great tact. And remember that life's a great balancing act. And will you succeed? Yes! You will, indeed! (98 and ¾ percent guaranteed). Kid, you'll move mountains." ~Dr. Seuss, *Oh the Places You'll Go!*

I WAS MOTIVATED to write *Climbing Your Inner Mountain* for a number of reasons. The most important was that I wanted to share what I had learned from my experience of climbing Mount Kilimanjaro: that anyone can reach his or her goals by overcoming external obstacles, negative mindsets, and difficult experiences. I believe that my experience can help each of us examine our spiritual journeys and explore how we create our worlds.

As an entrepreneur, I've seen, heard, experienced, and learned a lot of different principles that have contributed to the success of my career. Not only have those principles been instrumental to my business, they have also contributed heavily to my spiritual growth and who I've become as a person. In this book, I want to share key principles that were revealed to me during my seven-day odyssey on Africa's highest peak. The journey began as a tangible test of my mental and physical strength but ended up becoming a spiritual pilgrimage that changed my life for the better.

I already know what you're thinking: *Why in the world would a black man want to go to Africa for the sole purpose of climbing a mountain? Isn't that kind of thing reserved for eccentric white outdoorsmen?* You do hear about black people going on African safaris and business trips and getting in touch with their roots on the continent—but a mountain, a 19,500-foot mountain, at that? The answer is very simple: the climb had been on my bucket list—better yet, my life list—since I had taken African History classes in college.

I read about Mt. Kilimanjaro, and it was kind of a cool thing to say, "One day, I will climb it." But it was like a kid saying, "I'm gonna be Superman one day." I was never serious about it until I started talking to my friend Steve Myen about the planning that it took to climb a mountain. He had climbed a few mountains in his life, but nothing of Mt. Kilimanjaro's magnitude. We began to talk about Kilimanjaro for many subsequent years, but every year, I would chicken out just before I had to make travel plans and preparations for the climb.

I will readily admit that fear and thoughts of death played definitive roles in my procrastination, because all my life, I have suffered from asthma. Because of my ailment, people have always tried to put limits on what I could accomplish. Yet, even when fear was present, I have always set out to prove to myself and the naysayers that I could do what they said I couldn't. Yet, the thought of climbing one of the highest mountains in the world and the thought of all the folks who had died trying to do so were more than a little intimidating. I was scared to death. Then, in 2009, the unthinkable happened. My friend Steve was killed in a bizarre and tragic boating accident. At that point, I finally got serious about the goal we had discussed for so many years. I vowed to climb Mt. Kilimanjaro in Steve's honor.

I didn't know what I would experience, climbing the mountain. I literally didn't have a clue, but I did know that it was something I wanted to do because no one ever thought I could. By January 2011, when I actually made the climb, I was physically prepared for the task, but there was no way I could have trained for what I was destined to experience on that mountain. From the moment I looked up at the massive abundance that is Mount Kilimanjaro, I knew that I would be transformed. But I didn't know that inwardly I'd have to die before I could reach the top.

Even though I had set out to climb Kilimanjaro, the process forced me to "Climb Myself." I was forced to face many external obstacles that required me to look deep within myself to find solutions. I was engaged in an epic struggle that taught me more about who I really was. In retrospect, I see that the process actually began long before I traveled to Tanzania and set my feet at the base of the mountain. Even before I began my physical training one year before the climb, I realized that overcoming old fears and dealing with new discoveries about myself would be part of the process.

One day, as I sat alone in my office, I found myself staring at an African sculpture that Steve had given me. It depicted people stacked on top of each other all the way to the top. It seemed to me that the people were trying to climb over one another to make it to the summit—just as we see every day in the business world and in our social lives. As I thought about Steve and the positive example he had set, I began to wonder, *Is success really about us trying to climb over each other, or should we just focus on trying to climb ourselves—to reach the peaks of our own potential by climbing our own "Inner Mountains," if you will?*

I'm convinced that climbing our own *Inner Mountains* is the ultimate challenge. Reaching *that* peak is the true definition of success. If we all made this our priority, there would be no need to climb over anyone else. As individuals, we would already be in position to be the best person for any task. There is a mountain for everyone to climb. Some people climb physical mountains like Everest, Kilimanjaro, and McKinley. But we all face life mountains, whether it is building a business, finding a way to send our kids to college, or figuring out how to get through to our spouses.

The principles that became clear to me as I scaled Mount Kilimanjaro will help you conquer your toughest life mountain—no matter how high, no matter how rugged it might be.

1

GET READY

"Before anything else, preparation is the key to success."
~Alexander Graham Bell

How to Reach the Mountaintop?
The Secret's in the Basement

OFTEN, WHEN PEOPLE come to my house, the first thing they see is the expansive, elaborate structure with a three-car garage and the nice selection of cars within. They immediately comment on how beautiful the exterior of my home is. They then come inside and see all of the various awards and trophies that I have displayed throughout my home. They all want to know how I've managed to accomplish these things, and my answer is always the same: "The secret's in the basement."

It never fails: they always ask, "What do you mean, 'the secret's in the basement'?" And that's when I lead them to my basement and divulge my little secret. In the center of my basement stands a massive white wall that runs the length of the house. My guests never fail to look puzzled when I show them this otherwise ordinary-looking wall—until I explain the meaning behind my seemingly cryptic response. Within the confines of the wall in my basement, beneath the drywall, there is a four-foot slab of concrete. Under that is a steel beam that runs the length of the house, thus allowing that wall to act as a pivotal part of the foundation that supports the entire house.

Can you imagine building a tower without first building a solid foundation? It can be done, but the higher you build, the more unstable the tower would become, until eventually, all it would take is one misguided piece to cause the entire structure to come tumbling down. Such is life. In order to accomplish any major feat in life, you first have to have a solid foundation. With a solid foundation in place, you have positioned yourself to move safely upward to higher and higher heights. Building that foundation is a matter of getting your mind right, through intensive, systematic preparation.

Because I know that every major success begins in the mind, my process to climb Kilimanjaro began with a thought and then progressed to mentally visualizing myself standing at the top of the mountain with my arms raised triumphantly above my head in victory. Once that image was securely engraved into my brain, I had to mentally prepare myself for the one-year training I would have to endure in order to physically prepare my body for the task ahead. No problem. I completed my year of training, and then made it to the top of Kilimanjaro—this, despite the fact that I had never climbed a mountain before, despite the fact that I was still fighting a lifelong battle with asthma (often triggered by cold weather and strenuous physical activity), despite the fact that I had survived a health emergency on the way up. When I finally stood at the peak, with sub-zero temperatures and treacherous winds beating upon me, suffering from frostbite and exhaustion, but enjoying the panoramic view of Tanzania and Kenya that surrounded me, that initial image of triumph that inspired all of my preparation became reality.

At the same time, glimpses of other personal victories shot through my mind, victories that had started with visions of success and became real because I had diligently prepared then followed through on my plans. I thought about how I had once been a squatter in abandoned houses with my parents and siblings but went on to own luxury residences around the world. I thought about how I had gone from being hospitalized as a child after running one block to winning a scholarship to run track in college. I thought about the blue car with the red door that my family had driven while I was young; now, I have several classic, luxury vehicles in my garage. I thought about how I went from being an unwise college dropout to a self-taught entrepreneur, with expertise in deal-making and business management. And I thought about how I had used mental visualization, determination, and discipline to transform myself from a janitor in a Detroit factory to a self-employed real estate entrepreneur, enjoying an income well into seven figures. That humbling and sometimes painful three-year transformation was worth every bit of the struggle I had endured.

These thoughts were with me not only at the top of the mountain, but throughout my adventure to the top. As I describe the climb and my preparation for it, I will pause periodically and share a few flashbacks from my experiences in the basement of life—where I laid my foundation.

Before the Climb:
How a Mop and a Broom Prepared Me for Business

WHEN I WAS in my mid-twenties, after attending two different universities but leaving without a degree, I found myself working as a janitor for Ford Motor Company, sweeping and mopping floors in a huge auto plant. Although I was very entrepreneurial, I needed that job at the time to take care of my family. I got a job in the factory because it paid more than any other job or business venture available to me at the time. But I knew that I wasn't going to be there for long, so I needed to prepare as if I weren't a janitor. I needed to prepare as if I ran a multi-million-dollar business. I took that time as my time away, to get my mind together.

I came up with a strategy for making the best possible use of my time. As I pushed my mop cart around, I would listen to audio books. It was great. It seemed to me that during the three years I worked at Ford Motor Company, I got my PhD in that capacity. I was 100 percent focused. I got an MBA, listening to everything from Zig Ziglar to Wayne Dyer, Tom Peters, John Maxwell, and any of the popular motivational and business strategy authors you can think of. I poured myself into their study. The key to any form of preparation is discipline, and I knew I needed that kind of discipline. Listening to audio books got me prepared for the world of business and the life of an entrepreneur. As I pushed my mop cart, my supervisors and anyone else who saw me probably figured I was listening to hip-hop—Tupac, Dr. Dre, or Eminem. After all, I was a young, African-American guy, working in a plant. But I wasn't listening to any of that. I was studying. I was reading *Think and Grow Rich: A Black Choice* by Dennis Kimbro and Napoleon Hill, *Success Runs in Our Race* by George C. Fraser, *Why Should White Guys Have All the Fun?* by Reginald Lewis, and *The Goal* by Eliyahu Goldratt, a novel about plant management that I saw on the bookshelf of the Ford plant general manager's office. That book taught me about through-puts, and bottlenecks, and all the various business formulas. That's how I learned what other people studied in business administration classes in college.

There was a bookstore in Suburban Detroit called Talking Book World. I volunteered my time there for two months, just so I could get a membership. Richard Simtob, the owner, accepted my informal proposal. Over a two-month period, I helped Richard open new stores, and I even helped him design them. I poured my energy and enthusiasm into what Richard was doing and devoured every book Talking Book World had in stock. I literally listened to every audio book they had in the store related to business, entrepreneurship, self-help, or motivation. I studied. Imagine: I didn't turn my radio on for a whole year; I listened to nothing but audio books in my car. Every day's work was a total disciplinary program worth accomplishing. I was on fire, thirsty for knowledge. They say education costs, but ignorance costs more—a whole lot more. That period of preparation got me ready.

A buddy of mine and I started the 100 Book Club. There were about 10 of us, and our goal was to read or listen to 100 books a year. Only two of us made it. Statistics say that after finishing high school, the average person will not read one complete book for the rest of his or her life. My goal was to read two books a week. Using audio books, I read everything from self-help, to business, and marketing management—as much as I could put my hands on. By the time I left Ford Motor Company, I was trained. I was a walking business manual. I knew structure. I knew marketing. I knew etiquette. I knew how to present myself. I had studied so much that I had become the embodiment of all the books I had read. People would ask me questions, and without realizing it, my answers would be something I had read—all of that knowledge was a part of me.

Four Quarters to Prepare for the Mountain

STARTING AT THE bottom and moving methodically to the top had become part of my nature by early 2010, when I began physical training for climbing Mt. Kilimanjaro. The required training to prepare for the climb consisted of four stages; so I sought out advisors to help me every step of the way. During the first quarter, I had to bulk up with muscle, so I spent countless hours, five days a week, powerlifting to build mass and sculpt my body. I have to admit, I looked amazing after working out with my trainer. Afterwards, I had to change those bulky muscles into lean muscle, and that required lots of cardiovascular workouts. I spent the second quarter biking anywhere from 25 to 50 miles a day all around town through the rain, sun, sleet, and snow. I took breathing classes in the third quarter. Because of my asthma, breathing would become an issue for me on the mountain due to the changing levels of oxygen; so it was important for me to learn how to breathe properly. I embraced the teachings of the Tibetan Monks to learn the meditation, tandem, Raja, Kriya, Cobra, and Taoist breathing techniques that would allow me to control my mind, body, and spirit so I would be able to keep my asthma in check. Finally, I dedicated the fourth quarter to turning all of the heavy muscle I'd spent so much time building into fat that my body could burn during the climb. I spent the final months of my training eating pasta just about every day, six to seven times a day.

Late December in Africa

I WAS ABLE to convince my friend Tebebu Tsadik (Tib), a physically fit marathon runner from Ethiopia, to go with me to climb Kilimanjaro at the last minute. Things were shaping up well, and I was happy that I wouldn't have to go alone after all. Then, finally, there I was on the day before New Year's Eve, 2010, in Tanzania, getting ready to embark upon one of the most significant experiences of my life. I was both excited and apprehensive. I had purposely chosen that particular time to travel because I wanted to experience the 2011 New Year's celebration in Africa, and it was important to me to start my New Year climbing the mountain.

The trip for the seven-day climb was organized so that we had to go somewhere for at least two days to relax, recover from jetlag, get acclimated, and prepare our minds for the climb. Tib and I flew into Ethiopia to visit his family and relax after our 14-hour flight from Detroit. We spent the next day getting massages, taking in the sights, relaxing, and meditating. Meditation is described as "continued thought, contemplation, or spiritual introspection." It is to the mind and spirit what a colon cleanse is to the body, in that it allows you to purge your mind of the cerebral toxins that ultimately poison your drive and prevent you from focusing on and achieving your goals. As I lay on the table, getting a deep-tissue massage from Helga, my massive Russian masseuse, I meditated on many things. First, I pondered why I had to come to Africa, the land of beautiful black women, to get a massage from a burly Russian woman! Then I began to reflect on everything that had ultimately led to my presence there at that moment: the idea, Steve's death, the endless hours of training, and my desire to see if I could really pull this thing off. I was filled with a mixture of emotions that ranged from the sadness of missing my friend to the apprehension of what to expect from the task we were about to undertake, as well as the excitement of the thought of achieving my goal.

On December 31, we took a three-hour flight to Tanzania to enjoy the African New Year's Eve celebration in all of its splendor. The brilliant display of color, exotic foods, and festive music, combined with the African culture, were enough to make me feel that we were definitely getting the New Year off to a great start.

Inner Mountain Introspective:
How You Can Prepare to Climb Your Mountain

SUCCESS DOESN'T HAPPEN overnight, nor does it happen by accident. Success happens because the one who achieved it prepared for it. Malcolm Gladwell talked about K. Anders Ericsson's theory on the 10,000-hour rule in his book *The Outliers: The Story of Success.* He wrote about the amount of time it takes to become a master of anything: *"The people at the very top don't just work harder or even much harder than everyone else. They work much, much harder."*

Take basketball greats Michael Jordan and Larry Bird for example. They both became legends because they were willing to work harder and longer than everybody else to stay at the top of their game. Both of these men would shoot an additional 1,000 free throws after each game. Prince, the innovative musician, is quoted as saying that it took 30 years for him to become an overnight success. Tiger Woods began golfing at the age of two and has gone on to become one of the greatest golfers of all time. The Beatles had more than 10,000 hours of playing time before they achieved any major success, and Bill Gates acquired more than 10,000 hours of programming experience by the time he reached his twenties. The list goes on.

All too often, we allow ourselves to be intimidated by sometimes real, but mostly imagined, obstacles, when in reality, if we just focused our minds on a plan of action or the proper way to execute, rather than how we MIGHT fail, our approach would be totally different. Most of the time, we are the biggest thing standing in our own way. For example: you didn't go after the job promotion because even though you know you're qualified, the boss MIGHT give it to someone else—so you just stick to your comfortable, dead-end job. Or maybe you're a runner who won't try out for the hurdles, because, even though it's always been your dream to run them, you're afraid that you MIGHT trip and fall. Then there's that business that you always wanted to start, but everyone's telling you that you're crazy. They say that things MIGHT not work out, so you should just stick to working a 9-to-5. And the list goes on.

Rather than coming up with reasons and excuses for why you can't do something, learn how to concentrate more on executing the plan of action. It all starts with positive thinking. After all, can't never could do anything. I challenge you to document one instance of a person becoming successful or achieving a momentous task without first believing that it was possible. Every great success story begins with the thought, *I can do it.* After that, comes preparation.

Henry Ford once said, "The man who thinks he can and the man who thinks he can't are both right." Which one are you?

INNER MOUNTAIN JOURNAL

WHAT GOALS DO YOU WANT TO ACCOMPLISH? WHAT'S STOPPING YOU? HOW CAN YOU PREPARE TO REACH THEM?

_____

_____

_____

_____

_____

_____

_____

_____

_____

MOUNT KILIMANJARO

2

BEAT THE FEAR OF GETTING STARTED

———— ◆ ————

"I must not fear. Fear is the mind killer. Fear is the little death that brings total obliteration. I will face my fear. I will permit it to pass over me and through me. And when it has gone past, I will turn the inner eye to see its path. Where the fear has gone, there will be nothing. Only I will remain."
~ Frank Herbert

BEFORE THE CLIMB:
I NEEDED TO COME BACK FROM A SETBACK

I HAD LEARNED a great deal and experienced great success as a real estate investor, mortgage broker, mortgage lender, and political fundraiser after I'd left my job at Ford. But as I welcomed the new year of 2011 in the shadow of Mt. Kilimanjaro, I was facing one of the toughest periods of my life. My business and finances had been rocked by the real estate crash that followed the financial crash caused by Wall Street speculators in the fall of 2008. Back in 2007, at age 38, my real estate portfolio had reached a value of $250 million. I owned the world headquarters of companies like Lockheed. But during the first nine months of 2009, I had lost millions in residential real estate—every residential property I owned. The residential mortgage industry, which was the foundation of my business, had completely disappeared. Thankfully, I still had 100 percent of my commercial real estate, and every bit of it was occupied. My commercial portfolio included a two-million-square-foot building with General Motors Corp. as the prime tenant. But falling market values had cut the value of my commercial portfolio by more than half.

My business challenge was further complicated by personal attacks against me that were tied to a political scandal that I had nothing to do with in my hometown of Detroit. The impact of it all was weighing on me as New Year's Eve arrived and 2011 dawned. But it was time to beat the fears and overcome the doubts I faced as an entrepreneur still fighting through a worldwide Great Recession. With all of this in my head, climbing Mt. Kilimanjaro was a way for me to challenge myself, to retool myself, to see what I was made of. I knew that I was greater than the circumstances I faced. Mt. Kilimanjaro helped me set my sights higher and recognize that I could still go on. Although the crash of the financial and real estate markets had knocked the wind out of me, I was definitely not dead.

CLIMBING KILIMANJARO

DATE:
January 1, 2011

TEMPERATURE:
80°

ALTITUDE:
5718 ft. above sea level

LUNCH:
Smoked beef, vegetables, queen cakes, and chocolate Cinnabons

DINNER:
Leek soup and tilapia

A Visit from the Guide

THE NIGHT BEFORE we were scheduled to go to the mountain, my guide Peter paid Tib and me a visit at the hotel to go over the details of what we needed to do and what we could expect once we got there. We then went through our gear to make sure we had everything we needed for the trip. Peter inspected everything from my underwear right down to the kind of socks I would wear, and he gave in-depth dissertations on things like wool vs. cotton as it related to how each would benefit us in the elements. He was that detailed, he explained, because we would experience every type of weather on the mountain. That bit of knowledge was a pivotal point for me, because in life, we experience every kind of weather—with respect to the highs and lows of simply existing. That led me to wonder, *What would the world be like if people spent more time equipping themselves with the proper gear for the full range of life's experiences?*

Once my guide had finished preparing us for the next morning's departure, we were left alone to rest because we had to be to bed early; we would leave at 6 a.m. Unable to force myself into bed right away, I walked outside my hotel and stared at the African sky as it lit up brilliantly with fireworks from the New Year festivities that were still going strong. I began thinking about what the next morning would bring. Everything I had trained for over the past year all led up to this moment, and I still couldn't help but wonder if I was really ready for it.

As I lay there in what I knew would be my last comfortable sleeping accommodations for the next seven days, the weight of what I was about to do came crashing down on me, and I began to question myself. What if I couldn't do it? What if I got up there and my asthma started acting up? What had I gotten myself into? What if I didn't make it back? All those questions echoed in my mind, but then I began to ask myself just the opposite: What if I *did* do it? What if I got up there and my asthma *never* acted up? What if I *did* make it back? I would have accomplished yet another goal that I had set for myself that nobody thought I would be able to achieve. That particular thought was enough to usher me into a peaceful sleep, sprinkled with visions of myself standing atop the highest peak on the African continent with my arms triumphantly raised above my head in victory.

STARING DOWN FEAR ON THE MOUNTAIN

TAKING ON THE physical challenge of the mountain climb and staring yet another kind of fear down to size was my next challenge. New Year's Day 2011 was the big day. I woke up at 5 a.m., took a shower, and thanked God for the water—this would be the last shower I would take that week. After my shower, I packed my backpacks with water, energy/mineral-replacement drinks like Gatorade, juice and fruit bars, four pairs of underwear, five pairs of socks, a warm t-shirt, a pair of boots, and everything else I needed for the weather on the mountain. And of course, I couldn't leave without my iPod and iPad. After all, I needed something to do in case I got bored.

Once my bags were packed, I took another moment to reflect on what I was about to do. I was excited on one hand; on the other hand, I was like, "Holy guacamole!" Through the excitement, a level of nervousness existed because I didn't know what to expect. After all, I was a businessman, not a mountain climber. To top it all off, I'd heard that the weather was really cold up there, and I hated cold weather with a passion. Cold weather often restricted my lungs; so that led to thoughts of how I would get to a hospital if something did go wrong. I knew that I had the right mental attitude, but I began to question whether I was physically in shape enough to go the distance.

I definitely did not plan for my story to end on a distant mountain, thousands of miles from home. Before I left the U.S., I had sat my children down and told them that this was a long-held dream that I wanted to pursue, and that if they have big dreams, they should go for them. I joked with them about the possibility of dying during the climb but promised them that I would certainly be back. It is one thing to get hit by a car or to be a victim of a plane crash, but to climb a mountain and not make it—that would be embarrassing! I didn't want to go out that way.

Reality soon kicked in, and I stopped entertaining scattered thoughts. I remembered that I'd come all this way for one reason: to climb Mt. Kilimanjaro. There was no way I was turning back now. It was finally time to go. As we drove to the mountain site, I blasted James Brown, Dr. King's "I've Been to the Mountaintop" speech, Al Green, Frankie Beverly, J. Moss' "We Must Praise," and Eminem's "Lose Yourself" on my iPod to get myself hyped up. When we finally pulled up to the foot of the mountain, there stood Kilimanjaro in all of its glorious splendor, standing majestically at 19,500 feet above sea level. And here I was, about to climb it.

Prior to arriving in Tanzania to climb Kilimanjaro, I never thought about what it would be like to stand at the foot of the mountain; I only visualized myself standing at the top. As I looked up at this thing from our vehicle and realized how huge it was, I asked myself, "How am I going to climb this thing?" Every time I looked up, I felt more overwhelmed. It was obvious to me then that fear was what had caused me to put the trip off for so long. In order to get my thoughts back on track, I had to remind myself of the stories of others who had put their fears aside in order to do great things, the stories of Harriet Tubman, Dr. Martin Luther King, and President Barack Obama.

When I actually arrived at the starting point to begin my climb, I still had no idea what to expect because I only had what I had read and what others had told me to go by. But as I stood there at the foot of that mountain, looking up into the sky, unable to see where it ended, it scared me. It scared me to the point where I was almost physically unable to stay on my feet. I had to lie down and take a nap to keep from passing out. I stretched out for a 45-minute nap on a nearby bench just to calm my nerves. After I awoke, I closed my eyes, I prayed, and I drank some hot cocoa. Then I was ready.

Rite of Passage Dinner

ON THAT FIRST day, we climbed for a total of six hours. When we reached our campsite, I was tired, but I felt great. I had made it through my first day of climbing Mt. Kilimanjaro. I felt so good that I joined the porters in our make-shift kitchen and started slicing and dicing onions and garlic for dinner. I felt like I was Kilimanjaro's top chef. Later that evening, as we all gathered together around the campsite, the Masai warriors sang songs for us in Swahili. The Masai are known for their valor and bravery as well as their age-old customs and ability to thrive in arid lands. To hear them sing their songs for us was an honor. The songs were those of inspiration, freedom, and triumph about how the Creator had chosen me to climb that mountain. They sang, "You are one with the mountain. The ancestors are behind you. The ancestors are pushing you." The songs were so moving that by the time the men were done singing, I actually had tears in my eyes. It was a very magically majestic and emotional time.

The six-hour climb of the first day was just a physical feat. But during that evening meal, listening to the songs and stories of the Masai warriors, I was reminded that climbing a mountain was a traditional rite of passage for many young men on their way to manhood. Although I was already an adult with young-adult children, I recognized that climbing Mt. Kilimanjaro was my rite of passage. But I was not climbing just for Robert Shumake; I was climbing for my legacy. I was climbing for my children—to prove to them that they could achieve their dreams; if they focused and set their sights, they could do anything. I was climbing for my business, and I recognized that although the market had hit me hard, it didn't take my mindset or my vision. I knew I still had a brilliant mind; I could create anything. I was climbing for my community, because I recognized that when I talked to my black friends about climbing Mt. Kilimanjaro, they said, "You're the only person I've met who ever *talked* about climbing it, much less followed through and did it." I had the prayers and admiration of people cheering me on from my community. All of those thoughts propelled me and made me dig deeper.

INNER MOUNTAIN INTROSPECTIVE:
PROCRASTINATION IS A SYMPTOM OF FEAR

PROCRASTINATION IS THE killer of dreams. It is a symptom of fear. Losing my friend Steve in the midst of our plans to embark on the mountain-climbing adventure together taught me the value of living life to the fullest. As we all know, tomorrow is not promised to anyone. Today is a gift and should be treated as such.

How many times in your business or personal life have you found yourself talking about what you "want to do" or what you're "gonna do," only to turn around and allow yourself or someone else to talk you out of it with all the fearful "what-ifs?" In my last book, *For Entrepreneurs Who Considered Suicide When Business Got Tough!,* I wrote about the "I'm Gonna" Tribe vs. the "Never Say 'Die'" Tribe. I recommended that you take the time to ask yourself which category you fall into. Are you always talking about what you're "gonna do," or are you actively taking steps to make what you want to see happen, happen? What you're "gonna do" will never matter until it's done, and tomorrow never comes. There is only today. So stop procrastinating! Every day that you procrastinate in pursuing your dreams, they die a little. Carpe Diem! Now is the time to ask yourself, "To which tribe do I belong?" That's what I had to do at the bottom of Mt. Kilimanjaro.

We gathered at the base with 18 guides and assistants who carried the supplies to make our meals, pitch our tents, and handle other necessities. Then, before we knew it, we were off. The journey had officially begun. Oddly enough, after we began to climb, that paralyzing fear began to fade away more and more with each step I took toward my destination. That's how it is: the hardest part of any task is getting started, and once you get started, the rest seems to fall into place.

As we traversed the base, there was nothing but vast greenery, peppered with the most beautiful flowers I'd ever seen. The mixture of colors and hues was amazing. The weather was a balmy 80 degrees, and we all felt great. Everyone was in high spirits, telling stories of who they were and where they'd come from, and I began to relax a little.

INNER MOUNTAIN JOURNAL

To which tribe do you belong? Write out your plan to overcome your fear.

_____

_____

_____

_____

_____

_____

_____

_____

_____

_____

Day 1

PREPARATION: JUST GETTING STARTED

TIB AND ME AT THE BASE OF KILIMANJARO

3

OVERCOME EVERY HARDSHIP

"Those who are quite satisfied sit still and do nothing; those who are not quite satisfied are the sole benefactors of the world."
~ Walter Savage Landor

BEFORE THE CLIMB:
ATTACKED BY THE MEDIA, SMEARED IN THE MARKETPLACE

COMPETING IN THE world of business is tough enough; what you don't need is unnecessary controversy that follows you like your own personal raincloud everywhere you go. My raincloud, in the two and a half years before the mountain climb, was my association with former Detroit Mayor Kwame Kilpatrick, who resigned from office in September 2008 after pleading guilty to two counts of obstruction of justice. Controversy surrounding Kilpatrick's nearly seven years in office touched anyone who had ever worked closely with him, and that included me.

My whole business got tied up in dirty politics. Working with the Kilpatrick Administration was great, but it was toxic. After the mayor was forced to resign in September 2008, anyone who was affiliated with his administration was attacked through the media and through litigation. I supported Kilpatrick when he first ran for mayor in 2001. We were both young and energetic. I'm sure he saw some of himself when he saw my ambition and drive. With valuable connections to President Bush, governors, prime ministers, and other influential people around the world,

I became one of Kilpatrick's top fundraisers, and that gave me access to new opportunities after he won the election. I became a partner to both of the city of Detroit's retirement funds: the general employee's pension fund and the police and fire officers' pension fund. The boards of both funds invested a total of $70 million into my projects and ideas.

After the mayor's scandal hit, I was interviewed by the Securities and Exchange Commission, the FBI, everybody. I came out of those investigations unscathed, but I took media hits. The local media tried to sensationalize the fact that I had managed public funds and had also raised money for Kilpatrick. Their inference in every story was that I, as a young, black man who did not have a college degree, was unqualified to do what I had been doing. In their eyes, I had only been there because of my "hook-up" with the mayor. Never mind that the investments I had managed for the city pension funds were solid, making money, and providing verifiable returns—I wasn't qualified. For instance, the media suggested that an honorary doctorate I had received from Detroit's Lewis College of Business was something I had made up. The reality was that the college had gone out of business and had closed approximately five years after granting me the honor.

I was a real person, not a character on some TV show or a clown in the media circus. But the media treated me as if I were part of a comedy series or reality show. Their lies affected my family, my business, my livelihood. It's tough when you know the truth and you've still got to endure being judged and critiqued by people who don't know what you know. Dirty media and dirty politics created a situation in which I felt I was only being tolerated, not celebrated. Forget the fact that I had helped over 10,000 kids in this town, all the scholarships I'd given, all of the contributions to all of the political campaigns, from local, to statewide, to national—none of it really mattered. Most of those people who had once welcomed me but later rejected me were not authentic; they only wanted me for what they could get from me. So I lost a lot of fake friends and gained some real friends. It was frustrating. In any war, people throw grenades. You might not have gotten hit by the grenade, but shrapnel will kill you, too. I got hit by shrapnel. It didn't kill me, but damage was done.

Going through that experience cost me millions of dollars in legal fees, lost business, and my reputation. Because I was a father with kids in college, I had to sit down and be honest with them. I had to explain to them that Pops had taken a financial hit and that extra money was not going to be available for a while, beyond paying for their tuition and books. But I never lost who I was. The marketplace experience made me tougher. Pain in your life can be a rite of passage. Every person who has been through something can be greater on the other side.

Climbing Kilimanjaro

DATE:
January 2, 2011

CAMPSITE:
Shira

TEMPERATURE:
50°/80°

ALTITUDE:
11,300 ft. above sea level

BREAKFAST:
Fried eggs, porridge, oats and fruit

LUNCH:
Mushroom soup, boric sandwiches, vegetables, pasta and fruit

DINNER:
Zucchini soup, bread, rice, fruit and vegetables

SHUMAKE BOOM-BAH-YAY: WE CAN BE ANYTHING

THE NEXT MORNING on the mountain, I woke up to a biting cold that hit me like a closed-fisted punch to the face. Gone was the warm, balmy weather that had ushered me into a peaceful sleep only a few hours before, and in its place was a bitter taste of Mother Nature, swooping in to give me a swift reality check as to what lay ahead.

Even though it was cold, I was still warmed by the invigorating thoughts of the things I'd witnessed the day before: the beauty of the mountainside landscape, the clear starlit skies, and the power of the Masai Warriors' songs of freedom, inspiration, and triumph. Brother John, whom I also called "Smiling John" because he smiled every morning with a coffee-stained, chipped tooth (the best smile I ever saw), had issued the 7 a.m. morning wakeup call. We all vacated our tents and took what could only be described as bird baths to prepare for breakfast. As Americans, most of us never give a second thought to what a privilege it is to be able to take showers and baths at will in our nice heated homes with indoor plumbing. But out there on Mt. Kilimanjaro, I will never forget how it felt to have to bathe myself from a small basin of hot water with wet wipes in the freezing cold.

During breakfast, my spirits were still very high. I had eaten well, still felt relatively clean, my asthma was still in check, and I had taken the medicine that was required for my body to adjust to the changing altitude. I was ready to climb. We started out that morning at about 9,000-10,000 feet above sea level, and we were scheduled to climb a total of six hours that day. As we prepared to set off for the day's journey, I began to hiccup uncontrollably, but I paid it no mind as I eagerly followed my group. Later in the day, though the conditions were still relatively mild, I noticed that I was still hiccupping. It turned out that I was having an allergic reaction to the altitude medicine; so I had to endure the rest of the day's climb with hiccups that plagued me every 30 seconds to two minutes.

The higher we went, I noticed that there was less green, and the shapes of the trees began to change because there was less oxygen. That's right, less oxygen! And here I was, an asthmatic with a severe case of the hiccups. Benny, one of my guides, noticed my predicament, and he began to walk with me. He talked to me along the way, doling out words of encouragement, telling me that I could do it no matter what. Having someone that I barely knew there to encourage me in that way was very powerful for me. Even though I knew that they had taken many others along this very same course, he told me that there were very few African-Americans who had ever done it. The Masai men were excited about seeing one of their own, back at home, climbing. That was one of the many things that helped me to keep moving forward. I reminded myself that I was climbing for more than myself. All of a sudden, I felt like Muhammad Ali when he fought his epic championship fight against George Forman in Zaire, buoyed by the chants of, "Ali, boom-bah-yay (Ali, beat him)!"

"Shumake, boom-bah-yay" began echoing through my mind. At that moment, the hiccups didn't matter because I was there to climb Kilimanjaro, and that's what I was going to do. Come hell or high water, asthma or hiccups, I was getting to the top of that mountain. Still high from the excitement of it all, and by the grace of God, I made it through the six-hour climb. When we finally settled at Camp Shiri for the night, I was still hiccupping irrepressibly. I had to stick my finger down my throat to force myself to throw up the medication. That approach was a little unique, but I'm glad I did it. I had to do it. Once I did that, I felt 1000 percent better.

That night, I felt empowered as I sat in the tented kitchen, helping the cook prepare our dinner. I really enjoyed the process. I had conquered day two and survived the challenge of the hiccups, and Kilimanjaro's top chef was at it again.

CLIMBING THE STAIRS, AVOIDING THE HOLES: METAPHORS FOR OVERCOMING

I HAD SPENT the day talking philosophy with the Masai men. We discussed wisdom, food, music, politics, and eventually, what all men talk about: women. We laughed and laughed, and then the conversation turned to the more serious matters of church, Christ, nature, and the conflicted ethics of missionaries who came to the Motherland to give Africans the Bible and take their minerals and other precious resources and rob their continent. We shared our stories and points of view and developed a sort of kinship as we climbed.

During our discussion, I shared with them that I believed that everything required a choice. My salvation had required a choice, commitment requires a choice, life requires a choice. To blossom, to excel, to soar—or to sit on a stoop and do absolutely nothing while others climb mountains—all require choices. I told them that people are reflections of whatever circumstances they choose. "Whatever the circumstances," I said, "you can succeed. You can be a porter, a cook, or become president of this nation because you choose to do so."

At first, I was met with a lot of negativity because they all saw me as a successful businessman; so who was I to talk about hardship to a porter in Tanzania who had to live on $20 a month? I explained that poverty exists in every country, but also, in every country exists people who have fought to overcome. I was no different than the Masai men, no better. I too once lived in unfavorable conditions, but I overcame because I chose to do so, just as they too can choose. The more we talked, the more positive their outlook became on what I was saying, which allowed them to begin changing their choices.

"Life, for me, ain't been no crystal stair," a quote made famous by Langston Hughes, became an epiphany for me during my second day on the mountain. I was stepping over boulders, shrubs, and cracks, all the while, making my way up from the bottom—the hole in the valley—to the top of the mountain, where the light shined the brightest. The steps I was taking were actually stairs that had holes in them, the holes in the mountain, and these holes were the small hardships that I was experiencing. The hiccups, as an example, were a hardship that I had to overcome in order to reach my destination, and that helped me realize that there is light in every hole.

That night, before I went to sleep, I reflected on my life and growing up as a little kid, not having all the things that I wanted but still having to continue to climb in order to move forward. As I thought about biblical references, the thought occurred to me: *maybe that's why they call it the* Holy *Bible*—for every dark situation, there is always light shining through its pages to help you conquer.

As I prepared to go to sleep that night, my mind was rejuvenated as I took in all of the beauty that surrounded me. The African sky was free of pollution. I could see the stars so clearly that it felt like maybe I could pluck one right out of the sky and take it home with me.

Inner Mountain Introspective:
Overcome the Obstacles, Seek the Light

IN EVERYDAY LIFE, there are always hardships or holes that keep you from accomplishing your goals, but we have to remember that in every crack, a glimmer of hope appears. Whether your hole is a failed business, relationship, or physical challenge, if you look deep enough into that hole, you will see the light fighting to make its way through. For instance, the key to any business is doing small things: opening a bank account, sitting down with a lawyer or with an advisor. If you are serious about a business, you will do those small things. The obstacles we perceive as we climb our Inner Mountains make us stumble only because we take our eyes off the goal and let something small stop us.

When determining how we will conquer our individual mountains, we must determine our path and take responsibility for our successes as well as our failures. We can recognize the light breaking through, fill the holes with the steps of our personal progress, then lift ourselves to the next level of our journeys.

INNER MOUNTAIN JOURNAL

WRITE DOWN HARDSHIPS YOU HAVE OVERCOME IN THE PAST SIX MONTHS:

_____

_____

_____

_____

_____

_____

_____

_____

_____

DAY 2

OVERCOMING HARDSHIPS: LOOKING FROM WHERE I WAS TO WHERE I WANTED TO GO ON DAY TWO OF MY CONQUEST, I WAS OVERWHELMED, BUT I OVERCAME.

4

KEEP MOVING FORWARD

———◆———

"To succeed, you need to find something to hold on to, something to motivate you, something to inspire you." ~ Tony Dorsett

BEFORE THE CLIMB:
EVERYBODY NEEDS A MICHAEL WILCOX

AS THE POP music diva Beyoncé recognized when she named her boisterous on-stage personality Sasha Fierce, we all need an alter ego. I really believe that. When J.C. Penney was starting out in the retail business, he didn't have a collections department for his five-and-dime store; so he would pretend to be somebody else and make the collection calls himself. In his mind, J.C. Penney was a friendly neighborhood merchant; his alter ego was a tough hard-liner who demanded money from people who owed the kind-hearted Mr. Penney. Your alter ego can easily do things that seem hard to you in real life. Just remember what happens to Clark Kent when his alter ego goes into action!

Before I made my first major real estate investment, I developed an alter ego who was not Superman, but he was about as close as you could get to superhuman. I was a janitor who wanted to be a multi-millionaire. I wasn't at that place just yet, but "Michael Wilcox" was. He had everything I didn't have, and he gave me time to learn what he knew and build my competencies. Michael Wilcox was larger than life. Michael Wilcox had a Rolex watch. Michael Wilcox had a private plane.

Michael Wilcox had it all. He was smooth, confident and driven, and he had no fear. Michael Wilcox would never, ever take "no" for an answer. This guy was my confidence builder.

I created him during a phone call to a property owner named Mr. Bradfield. I wanted to apply what I had learned about negotiating tactics, but I didn't want to make any mistakes as Robert Shumake. So when I asked to speak to Mr. Bradfield, and the receptionist asked me, "Who's calling?" my answer was, "Michael Wilcox." His name, his personality, and all of his attributes came to me right on the spot.

I bought that property, my first big real estate deal, after Michael Wilcox had convinced Mr. Bradfield to drop his price from $40,000 to $18,000. When we met to sign the purchase agreement, I had literally left for lunch from the Ford factory. I ran out the door wearing my work smock.

When I arrived to sign the papers, and after sharing the truth about my identity, I let Mr. Bradfield remind me that cash needed to change hands. "Mr. Shumake, I need a deposit, or something," he'd said.

Using all of my negotiating tactics, I reached into my pocket and gave him a dollar. That was all I had in my pocket. He laughed, but he took it. I told him, "I'm going right to the bank to get financing."

The bank gave me $28,000 because my negotiations with Mr. Bradfield had given me that much equity in the property. I had done other business transactions where I was paid in cash (promoting parties and the pager business, for instance), but this was my first experience being paid a substantial amount with a check. From my viewpoint, I had entered "the check world." I took the check to the bank and cashed it, just so I could see all of the cash on the table, just so I could grasp and crack the stack of tightly wrapped bills and hold them in my hand—then I put the money right back in the bank. One dollar down had produced a $10,000 profit. That was a great return on my investment. I got the bug after that. I said to myself,

Man, I can get out of my job at the Ford plant. I can do this fulltime!

My next move was to get a real estate auction book from a professional real estate office. There were 2,300 homes in that book, and I looked at every last one of them in two and a half weeks. My shift started at 5:00 in the morning. When I got off in the afternoon, I would drive around and look at houses until I had to use a flashlight in the dark. I would get home at 2:30 or 3:00 in the morning, then get back up and go back to work. I was looking at lots in the middle of the night, writing what I needed to buy on a piece of paper and how I would buy it. The properties were all over Wayne County, Michigan.

Once I decided what I wanted, I cashed in my 401K and my bank accounts. I turned just about everything I had into cash. With real money in hand, I bought 40 pieces of property at one auction, in one day. From there, I kept going at a steady, determined pace. I started having fun with negotiating. The real-life role playing I did as Michael Wilcox made me a terror on the telephone whenever I negotiated a deal. When I had to deal with someone in person, I always *represented* Michael Wilcox, who couldn't make the meeting that day. In that position, I couldn't give in on anything, because Michael Wilcox was a relentless boss, who refused to accept bad news of any kind.

I bought lots that had fences around them. The fences usually belonged to a store owner. I would go to the store owner and say, "You've got to tear this fence down or buy my property from me." I might have paid $200 for the lot, but I would sell it for $20,000.

Once, when a friend of mine had bid on a property for me, I told her, "I want the property at this price, and I want the golf clubs in the basement as well." They were nice clubs, and I got them when the seller agreed to the deal. Those golf clubs were a testament to what I had learned and what I continue to believe: you don't get what you deserve in life; you get what you negotiate. I've been negotiating ever since. I only went after those golf clubs because I wanted the experience of bidding on them. When people buy houses, too often, they pay full price. Sometimes, they even pay more, fearful of being outbid by someone else. Too many of us even pay full price for cars, when the dealers are already prepared to negotiate. We take everything at face value, but we should stop doing that. We should negotiate—because everything is negotiable. You get more when you do it that way. I even negotiated with my barber. I told him I'd pay him six months in advance if he would give me twenty percent off the price. He took it.

I must have made $200,000 from all of the property I bought that single day at the real estate auction. During this period in my life, I was in the habit of looking in the mirror and telling myself that I was great. I talked about succeeding and success around the clock. As I spent more time in that space, Robert Shumake and Michael Wilcox began to integrate into one. We began as a negotiating team, but eventually became the same person.

CLIMBING KILIMANJARO

DATE:
January 3, 2011

CAMPSITE:
Barranco

TEMPERATURE:
30°

ALTITUDE:
12,500 ft. above sea level

BREAKFAST:
Porridge, cucumbers, tomatoes, papaya, beef sausage, eggs and toast

LUNCH:
Jacket potatoes, cream of mushroom soup and spaghetti

HELP FROM A SPIRITUAL GUIDE: GO DEEP WITHIN YOURSELF

THE THIRD DAY of our excursion saw the temperature drop from 80 degrees to 15 degrees at 13,000 feet above sea level. That day, we climbed for a total of seven hours, and during that time, the landscape changed from the plush greenery that welcomed us at the start of our journey to an immense span of fog and rocky terrain. To make matters worse, the further we went, the harder I found it to breathe.

The chill I experienced at that altitude was so piercing that my teeth were chattering audibly and my bones began to ache. It was so cold and foggy that by the time we had set up camp and I climbed into my tent, I went into a full-blown asthma attack. Suddenly, my greatest fear was in front of me. First, I tried using my Albuterol inhaler, but it was freezing, and the cold air made it impossible for my lungs to expand enough for the medicine to get into them. When that didn't work, I tried to call the breathing techniques I'd learned in my training classes to the forefront of my memory, but it was to no avail. As the condition of my labored breathing became more intense, I felt as if a large man was slowly and purposefully squeezing the life out of my body. Nothing seemed to work, so I began to panic. I started to wonder if I was going to die on Mt. Kilimanjaro.

I think about death occasionally, and I can honestly say that I'm not afraid of it. But the bottom line was that I didn't want to die here. Not this way. In fact, I had told my children before I'd left that if I died on my trip, not to tell their friends that I had died climbing Mt. Kilimanjaro.

I'm gonna die ... I don't wanna die here ... I didn't come here to die ... these were my thoughts as I alternated between panic and trying to figure out the proper combination of breathing techniques to get air into my body. I really couldn't breathe. On a scale of 1 to10, the attack I was having was a 9.5. With an attack of that magnitude, I really needed to get to a doctor within 30 minutes for treatment. I was in a full-blown sweat by the time I called my guide to see if they could bring me some oxygen. They immediately sent someone to get some for me, and then I told him that I needed to get to a hospital and asked how long it would take. He explained that it would take six hours for me to climb back down the mountain to get to a place where I could catch a plane to Kenya, where the nearest hospital was located. My other option was to climb up the mountain another four hours to get to the top.

I was delirious as I continued to gasp for air. I could hear the Masai men frantically running to and fro, yelling into their walkie-talkies, "The black American is sick, the black American is sick!" In hindsight, it was a little comical that in a matter of 48 hours they had gone from singing, praising, and taking pride in the fact that a black American man had risen to the challenge of taking on this rite of passage to frantically trying to find some way to get me off that very same mountain.

Going back was not an option for me. In the grand scheme of things, I really didn't know how to go back—at any time, under any circumstances. Quitting had never been an option. I had come there to climb Kilimanjaro, and I would rather have died running toward my dream than to have died running away from it. If I was going to go, I wanted to do it my way—and I had come too far to turn back.

I don't want to die like this, I had told myself. So I sat there in my tent and began to do what I should have done in the first place: I went to the Creator. I began to pray, meditate, and praise Him. It was roughly 5:30 a.m. when the caretakers finally brought me some oxygen. Somewhere around that time, the Voice told me, "Go in your bag." There in my bag, I found various vitamins and supplements, and then something inside of me said, "Crush them." So I crushed them together in the palm of my hand and I began to suck on those while taking in the oxygen, and I continued to pray. It was at that moment that I found the proper breathing technique, and at that point, I knew that I would be okay.

Inner Mountain Introspective:
What Do You Do when You Have Nothing Left?

AFTER I HAD gotten through my asthma attack, a passage I had read from Rudyard Kipling's poem "If" popped into my head:

> *"If you can force your heart and nerve and sinew to*
> *serve your turn long after they are gone*
> *and so hold on when there is nothing in you except the*
> *Will which says to them: Hold on!"*

The magnitude of the statement had such an impact on me because I had just experienced it. It taught me that the sheer force of one's will is stronger than anything we could ever imagine. Take President Barack Obama for example: in the years before he became president, he couldn't get tickets to the Democratic Convention in the rafters; now, he is the leader of the free world. He didn't allow himself to be deterred by focusing on the odds that were stacked against him: being black, coming from a broken home, growing up poor; instead, he focused on his goals, accepted the challenge with gusto, and went on to run one of the most memorable presidential campaigns in history and win.

Muhammad Ali, certainly one of the greatest boxers in history, would use what was called the "rope-a-dope" fighting technique against his competitors to win fights. It was ingenious in that he would allow himself to become seemingly tied up in the ropes as he was mercilessly pummeled by his opponent, when in actuality, the ropes would absorb the bulk of the force while the opponent exerted his energy. All Ali had to do was endure until an opportunity presented itself. At that point, he would take advantage of his opponent's weakness to counterattack and go on to win the fight. Mind over matter—mind over circumstance.

When you recognize your purpose in life, all you're supposed to do is keep moving forward and let the Creator handle the rest. Push that fear aside and remember that if He brought you to the situation, He will surely bring you through it. The journey to get to your final destination may not always be easy. It may even be seemingly unbearable, but if you keep moving forward, even when you have nothing left to propel you but the sheer force of your will, He will give you what you *need* to make it through.

I remember one day while taking a drive, I saw a squirrel dart into the street a few yards ahead. From my car, I could see that there was a nice gathering of acorns in the grass on the other side of the street where the squirrel was headed, and he was going at a fast-enough pace that I had no worries about the animal being in any eminent danger—not from me, at least. As I continued to cruise along, all of a sudden, the squirrel stopped in the middle of the street to glance back at the side he'd just left. He looked back and forth from where he'd come from to where he was headed, as if trying to decide what to do. Did he want to leave the place he knew was safe, or did he want to move forward to claim the reward that the Creator had for him on the other side?

By the time the squirrel saw my car and I realized that he wasn't going to be able to move in time for me to miss him, it was too late. He had allowed fear of the unknown to make him shift his focus. So instead of moving forward toward his goal, he chose to focus on the past, and it ultimately cost him his life.

When I look back on the night of my asthma attack and being faced with the very real possibility of losing my life, I realize that if I had given in to fear and opted to go back—when God had given me a mission—I am fairly certain that I would have died that night. The old saying goes, "When the going gets tough, the tough get going." The ability to overcome starts with the will to do so. Again, the question: what do you do when you have nothing left? The answer: you put your trust in Him, and you keep moving forward.

INNER MOUNTAIN JOURNAL

THINK OF A TIME WHEN YOU HAVE HAD TO PUSH YOURSELF TO
THE LIMIT TO ACHIEVE A GOAL. HOW DID IT MAKE YOU FEEL?

_____

_____

_____

_____

_____

_____

_____

_____

_____

_____

DAY 3

KEEP MOVING FORWARD: TIB AND ME MAKING OUR WAY UP.
"DON'T SLIP!"

5

DARE TO HEAR A MOUNTAINTOP MESSAGE

———•———

"Although the world is full of suffering, it is also full of the overcoming of it." ~ Helen Keller

BEFORE THE CLIMB: BEATING FEAR, VISUALIZING SUCCESS: MY NEW YEAR'S EVE TRADITION

LONG BEFORE MY business success and political involvement, I used an annual ritual to help me beat my fears and eliminate limitations in my thinking. Call me superstitious, but since I was in my mid-twenties, I have spent New Year's Eve locked in a room, laying out plans and goals for the New Year. I would turn them over and over in my mind until they became so vivid that I could hear, taste, and smell the ideas as they formulated in my mind. My ambitions became so real to me in those moments that they actually took root in my soul. I prided myself on shutting out the rest of the world for that 24-hour period. On January 1, I would emerge from my self-imposed seclusion, ready to conquer the world. I became convinced that embarking upon any plan of action, business or otherwise, without a plan is like planning to fail.

When I didn't have much money, I would get a hotel room somewhere in Detroit for my New Year's Eve meditation. Since then, my New Year's tradition has taken place in other great cities around the world. This process led to the idea of buying real estate for corporations and the creation of my commercial real estate business. During that annual period of isolation and intense focus, I was able to come up with a concept, pull people together, and ultimately develop that business into a nationwide $250 million real estate enterprise.

My New Year's Eve meditation also helped me come up with an event that serves what I call my "double-line bottom line": making a profit while also making a difference. I created the Shumake Relays, a track meet that emphasizes scholastic achievement for children and gives back to inner cities. I grew that meet from 0 to 10,000 kids over a seven-year period, giving away more than $100,000 in scholarships to kids in the program. So I'm serious when I say that focusing on New Year's and shutting down—almost like a Zen monk—in order to accomplish your dream pays off. I'm a living testament that it works. Knowing this, I brought my usual New Year's Eve intensity to Tanzania and the foot of Mt. Kilimanjaro. I had to mentally and physically prepare for the task before me. That 24-hour period of seclusion on Dec. 31, 2010 allowed me to reflect on where I was in life and how I could recover from a year that had really knocked me for a loop.

CLIMBING KILIMANJARO

DATE:
January 4, 2011

CAMPSITE:
Karanga

TEMPERATURE:
20°

ALTITUDE:
13,500 ft. above sea level

BREAKFAST:
Porridge, toast, beef sausage, fried eggs, fruit and juice

LUNCH:
French fries, fried chicken, stir fried vegetables, pineapple and rice

There Are Always Inner Voices If We're Willing to Listen

SOMETHING HAPPENED ON that mountain, something that changed my life. Here I was in the wee hours of the morning on the fourth day of my climb, coughing, sneezing, drenched in sweat. I had just survived what must have been the worst asthma attack I had ever experienced. At the same time, I had made a powerful connection with God that jump-started what I referred to as my "spiritual sound system."

We were just past the halfway point and the real climbing hadn't even begun yet. After my asthma attack, I was still very cold, so Brother John and the other guides boiled water and gave me hot water bottles to put in my sleeping bag to help warm me up. Although my breathing had returned somewhat to normal, I was still wheezing and experiencing sharp pain in my chest. All alone up there on that mountain, I began to talk to God and all of His angels.

I said, "Lord, here I am. What do you have for me to do? I don't want to go out like this, but if I've got to go, at least I'll know I was going toward my dream. I'm not turning around and going back."

I had tried oxygen and every other remedy, and nothing was working. Then all of a sudden, I felt like a cool hand had touched my chest and taught me how to breathe slowly and actually calm myself down. I heard that Voice that you read about and hear about so many times. It said, "I've got you. You're going to be all right."

I knew then that I could climb that mountain. It gave me the ultimate confidence in the world. Here, I had survived my greatest fear: an acute asthma attack. It was so cold on the mountain that the medicine I was taking would not work. I was in a feverish sweat. I didn't take a shot and didn't go to the hospital, yet I was still alive and still on the mountain. There was still a long way to go, but at that point, I felt that if I didn't go any further, I had already won because I had conquered a fear I'd had for over 40 years.

Feeling that hand and hearing, "I've got you; it's going to be all right" were the most spiritual experiences that I'd had on the mountain. Because I was on a mountain like Moses and Jesus had been in scriptures, I sensed that I had had a mountaintop experience similar to theirs. I sensed I might have even had an encounter with Michael, the chief archangel identified in the Bible. My experience helped me to understand what it must have been like for Moses and Jesus to be tuned in with God on a mountain for 40 days and nights. It's no wonder they could move people and save the world.

Despite the wheezing and pain, I was ready to continue because I knew that God was going to help me get to the top of that mountain. I already felt as though I had died on that mountain, so if I would have died physically at that point it would have been okay.

That day, we started out around 9:00 a.m. instead of 6:30 a.m. My little mishap had caused a minor time delay, but in my mind, that didn't mean that we were off our journey. We climbed for five hours on day four, and I spent the first four hours marveling at the fact that I was still in the game. The discomfort and fear were like constant luggage, but my goal was to finish, so the luggage was just going to have to come with me because I wasn't going to let it stop me. I had moved beyond the physical person, because, quite frankly, I didn't have any physical strength left. There was nothing but pure spiritual and mental emotion left to drive me. In the business world, I am a businessman, a shot-caller. I am the man with a plan who makes things happen, but out there, I was only one millionth of a percentage of a massive structure that was made by the hands of the Creator. The contrast was very humbling, and again, I was left to wonder if I could do this. It was at this point that my spiritual sound system kicked into full blast. There was nothing there but me and the elements. I had forgotten all about everything and everyone else; it was just God and me.

Shh ... Be Quiet!

DURING MY INNER conversation with God, I reflected on all the different things that I could have done better, could have done greater. I thought of many things. I thought of my relationships with my children. I thought of my relationship with my parents. I thought of relationships with other loved ones. As a young entrepreneur, I had done well and created wealth and had been totally blessed; so to an extent, I was not as focused in my life as I could have been. Going through a market crash had taught me focus, but being on that mountain showed me plainly some squandered opportunities that I had missed—not because I wasn't looking, but because I was moving so rapidly, I didn't see those things. They were right in front of me and I had missed them.

As I climbed, it seemed that there was a spiritual Bose sound system functioning in my head. That resounding inner Voice pointed out mistakes I had made in life and in business as clear as chess moves. Three in particular were life-changing checkmates that I was too busy to see. I could hear God say, "You see these three things I've laid out for you?" I realized that despite all of my accomplishments, I had not yet maximized the talents I had been given. His message to me was that when I finished climbing the mountain, these were the things that he wanted me to work on. Finally, after a while with the Voice on full blast, it became punishing, deafening, and I found myself begging God, "Okay, okay! Turn it down! I hear you!"

Being on that mountainside made me recognize that I needed to make more time to put the rest of the world on mute so that I could have time with the Voice. It's amazing how when there wasn't a telephone or an iPad to distract me (because the batteries were completely dead), I had no choice but to focus on what God was showing me. I didn't even want to listen to my iPod because, at that time, it was just me and the Creator, and I wanted to hear everything He had to say to me.

That particular climbing session taught me to refocus on my dreams. My quiet time with God opened up a whole new world of possibilities for me about how I could become a better person and make a greater impact. As God spoke to me on Mt. Kilimanjaro, He gave me insight as to how He wanted to use me to impact the lives of others, while at the same time leaving something of real value behind for my children and my children's children. For me, that was a powerful thing.

I was broken on that mountain. My money meant nothing on that mountain. A car meant nothing on that mountain. What meant something was sharing a song or a great inspirational message. After God had allowed me to be broken down to the point where I had no choice but to listen to Him, he was able to show me things that I never would have been able to receive spiritually under normal circumstances. I realized that I had too many self-imposed distractions (i.e. phone, fax, email) clouding my spiritual eyes and ears.

That night, I'm just going to say it, I felt like I was the man! I felt like a hero. I had actually beaten asthma. I had beaten the thing that had kept me in and out of the hospital for most of my life, and I had done it right there on that mountain. I had been called the "bubble boy" and was forced to miss out on Christmas, New Year's, birthdays, and many other holidays because of my affliction. To be on a mountain and be able to conquer it and move on toward my dream was powerful. I had an internal cheerleading session with myself that night because people had counted me out. My guides had counted me out. I was the black American who'd gotten sick and whom they had tried to turn back. But I wouldn't go.

Even though I was physically depleted with seemingly nothing left to give, that night before I went to sleep, I felt like I was on top of the world.

INNER MOUNTAIN INTROSPECTIVE: MIRROR, MIRROR, ON THE MOUNTAIN

IMAGINE WAKING UP in the morning, brushing your teeth, putting on your clothes, getting in your car, and going to your first meeting without ever doing a mirror check.

On that mountain, there were no mirrors, so my mirror check was on the inside. The things that I had experienced up to that point had forced me to take a good look at myself as a person and evaluate who I was at the core. After a lot of intro-spection, I remembered that I was the son of the King and that His Word had promised that I could do ALL things through Christ who strengthens me. So I had to turn on the light in my mind, jump out of my fears, raise my soul, gargle my spirit, brush my nerves, clothe myself in victory, and give a high-five to the Creator so I could get back to climbing my mountain.

Success is no instantaneous experience. Accomplishment takes time. We live in a microwave society, where we want every-thing now. Technology has spoiled us to the point that the very thought of waiting for anything more than a few minutes brings about feelings of impatience and anxiety. In a world that revolves around hustle and bustle, and sometimes utter chaos, it's impor-tant for us to learn how to just sit back and be quiet sometimes. Can you imagine what our lives would be like if we all took more time out of our busy schedules to hear our Creator's voice? I'm not sure I would recommend 40 days and nights like our friends of the Old Testament, but if we take a few days out of our busy lives to truly listen to the Voice, we could undoubtedly make changes in a few lives, starting with our own.

INNER MOUNTAIN JOURNAL

Do you have a spiritual life? Do you think you need one? What day of the year will you set aside for yourself to listen, plan, and just be still?

_____

_____

_____

_____

_____

_____

_____

_____

_____

_____

DAY 4

SPIRITUAL BREAKTHROUGH: BY THIS TIME IT WAS GETTING PRETTY ROUGH ON KILIMANJARO.

6

FOCUS! PUSH YOURSELF TO THE FINISH LINE

"The only way of finding the limits of the possible is by going beyond them into the impossible." ~Arthur Clarke

Before the Climb: Moving to the Next Level

I HAD ENTERED a new world mentally and financially after I bought my first residential investment property from Mr. Bradfield. But a lingering belief that I should hold on to the predictability of a paycheck as long as I could kept me on the job at the Ford plant. They say pain sometimes is a motivator. It took a painful disgust with the work I was doing to finally drive me out of that building. There was a guy who worked at the plant who was lactose intolerant. I called him "The Diaper Man." He'd get something that had milk in it every now and then, and he would just go. He'd run to the bathroom and just blast the whole restroom out, terribly—feces on the wall, feces on the floor, feces on the back of the stall, feces on the mirror, feces everywhere. To this day, I can remember it vividly. It was everywhere. So as the janitor, I was supposed to go in there and clean up. I did it once, and then made up my mind not to ever do it again. I said to myself, _I can't clean up another man's crap. My life does not extend to cleaning up another man's crap._ After the first time, I wouldn't do it anymore. They called the union on me. I wasn't cleaning it up. That was a defining moment, and it happened not long after I closed that first real estate deal. *You know what, I can't do it,* I'd told myself. *There's a greater life for me.*

Many people start there and say, "I'm going to leave next year." Yet, they end up staying—long enough to get a gold-plated watch from the company. I wanted a Rolex watch. I knew that in order for me to achieve that, I had to leave the Ford plant. Waiting 30 years to get Henry Ford's gold-plated watch was not for me. Cleaning up another man's crap was not for me; so I finally left that job and started writing mortgages in addition to my core business of buying and selling real estate. I had a big goal: I wanted to make $200,000 a year writing loans and doing property. The most I had made at Ford Motor Company was $60,000, with all the overtime in the world. But I made $194,000 during the first year I focused on real estate.

I got a chance to apply all I had studied about marketing and process right there on the ground. The next year, I went from making $200,000 to $600,000 for the year. The year after that, I went to a million, and my business just kept growing. I knew I had been at Ford just a little bit too long. Albert Einstein said two objects containing mass cannot occupy the same space at the same time. There was a space in life for me. I needed to step into that. Somebody else needed that job I had at Ford. That was their dream. That wasn't my dream. I was just occupying space. They talk about Occupy Wall Street; I was just occupying Ford Motor Company, and I needed to get up out of there!

I went from being a mortgage broker to owning my own real estate company, First Equity Home Loans. I grew that business to about $80 million a year in mortgage volume, which is a decent-sized shop. Because of the political contacts I had developed, I went from that to managing real estate for the government and became the largest HUD broker in the state of Michigan by 1999. I controlled 85 percent of every piece of property sold under HUD in Michigan.

Meanwhile, I met Steve Myen and others in the commercial real estate business who had taught me that "the zero makes the difference." Even though I had begun to do deals that produced up to $1 million on a single transaction, they showed me that I could put in the same amount of effort and make *many* millions on each transaction. I had been in the real estate business for only a few years, but momentum was building and my life just started moving.

Climbing Kilimanjaro

Date:
January 5, 2011

Campsite:
Barafu

Temperature:
10°

Altitude:
15,239 ft. above sea level

Breakfast:
Oats, bread and potatoes

Dinner:
Rice, beef stew and vegetables

A Set Back Is a Setup for a Comeback

BECAUSE I WAS sick the day before, the plan on day five was to see if I could cut one day out of my trip by making it to the top that day so I could go back and be done with it, but it all depended on how I felt. It was at that point that my friend Tib and I made an agreement that if I didn't feel well enough to continue, he had to go on by himself.

Even though I was still high from the excitement of my personal victories, I still didn't feel 100 percent, but I managed to complete the five-hour climb to the next camp. I wasn't ready to take a shortcut, so Tib ended up going the rest of the way with Benny, our assistant guide, to the top, which was still another five hours away. I was happy for my friend as I watched him leave with the guide, and I fully expected the journey to be relatively easy for him without my significantly slower pace slowing him down. After all, he was a seasoned marathon runner and was in good shape. So while Tib climbed, I waited patiently for him at the campsite.

When he returned, I asked him, "How was it?"

The first words from his mouth were "It was horrible! It was terrible! It was the worst experience of my life!" He told me that he didn't want to talk, he didn't want to eat; all he wanted to do was go to bed. I looked closely at him for a moment, and his face was badly swollen. His eyes seemed to be rolling to the back of his head and he was clearly exhausted. Mind you, I had never run a marathon before and I wasn't in shape like he was. Plus, I'd just had a full-blown asthma attack, so you can imagine what was going through my mind at that point: If he had problems, how was I going to make it? That's when fear came back knocking at my door, and there I was again, doubting whether I could go the distance. Once again, my spiritual sound system kicked in. It said, "Look dude, you just beat asthma. You can do this thing." But immediately, I was back in the flesh, combating my spiritual reasoning with every excuse I could come up with: He's an athlete. He runs marathons. He's done all these different things … The list went on.

The Spirit said, "You beat asthma; you can do it. You beat the biggest obstacle in your whole life already. Surely, you can climb a mountain."

That was enough for me. That's when I devised a plan, because I know that every successful mission starts with a good plan. I determined that if I was going to make it to the top the next day, I was going to have to climb at night. So I ate a good meal and tried to block all of Tib's negative statements out of my mind. I decided that I was going to go as far as I could, and if I couldn't make it to the top, then that would be okay, but I wanted to at least be able to say that I gave it my best.

By now, we were more than halfway there and I had to force myself to come to grips with the fact that I was going to have to finish the journey alone. As I lay in my tent that night, a lot of things ran through my mind, the top three being the words of Tib and the fact that he was in the tent next to me, asleep and sore, my ever-looming asthma, and the fact that I had to be up in two hours to start climbing again.

Fear was no longer a luxury that I could afford, so I had to quickly get my mind right so I could get some rest. I knew that God was going to pull me through this experience, but the fact of the matter was that I didn't want to do it alone. Tib and I had been cheering each other along the entire time, and I took comfort in having my friend by my side. After all, who wants to go to a party alone?

My guide, Peter, and I got up in the still of the night and began climbing again at 10 p.m. It was only 10 degrees, and after two hours, I began to get frostbite in my fingers and toes. The cold was so piercing and painful that the only thing I could think to do was to take my gloves off and put my hands on my private parts, as we'd learned in the military, so that my body heat would restore some of the feeling in my hands.

I became a zombie to the sound of the thump, thump of one foot following the other. I constantly heard the words "pole, pole"—or "take it slow"—from Peter, urging me onward. As I tried deliriously to reach the "pole pole" pace, my eyes rolled to the back of my head and it seemed as if I was having an out-of-body experience. The discomfort in my hands and feet were of no consequence because I had to keep going, or else it all would have been for nothing.

Dead Man Walking

IMAGINE YOURSELF TRYING to accomplish a task without a deadline, and the time frame ranges from an individual who is in tip-top shape to one who is just average. You've heard the saying, "How do you eat an elephant?" The answer is simple: "One bite at a time." I don't know about you, but I don't eat elephant, so I couldn't imagine having to eat a whole one! But it became very clear to me that I wouldn't be climbing in any record time, so it would have to be done one brick, one stone, one step at a time.

By day five of my climb, I really felt like I was a dead man walking. Every inch of my body was screaming out in pain. My chest was on fire from the cold air mixed with my wheezing, and to top it all off, I had frostbite in my fingers and toes, and even through my boots, I knew that I had lost three toenails. But I couldn't think about that. At that point, it became all about focus. I was there to climb that mountain, and if asthma didn't kill me, I wasn't going to allow frostbite and lost toenails to do it either. Mind over matter.

Inner Mountain Introspective:
Make the Choice to Focus and Finish!

THE POWER TO focus throughout a task is crucial. Sometimes, the tasks that we have are overwhelming and we tend to get distracted and want to move on to something else, but we can't. People challenge themselves for many different reasons, but if they lack the ability to focus, the distractions or obstacles that lie within those challenges will always succeed in throwing them off track. If your goal is to accomplish a task, finish a business plan, apply for a job, or finish law school or medical school, you can't get distracted. At those times when it starts getting tough to keep your focus, you've just got to be a dead man walking in order to focus on the task at hand.

While climbing on day four, I noticed some unique-looking field mice running around the mountainside. They were called four-striped mice, and though they're common in various parts of Africa, this particular species was unique to high altitudes. It was shocking at first to see those mice up there on the mountain with me in those freezing conditions, but the real shock came when I realized that was as far as they could go. They couldn't survive at the bottom in the warmth and lush green pastures, and they couldn't go any higher because it was too cold for any vegetation to grow. They were created for the sole purpose of existing right where they were on that mountain. They didn't have the flexibility of surviving different climates. I had learned how to survive in a situation where I was able to transcend my obstacles, but here were these mice that were stuck because they couldn't go up or down.

There are so many people that at times need to move forward but don't, and then there are times when we need to go back, but we need to realize that we can't just stand still and be in the same place. We need to make choices. Whereas I had been given a choice to backtrack six hours for treatment or to go forward and up four hours to victory, the mice didn't have a choice. They had to be content with merely existing where they were or die.

At times, when you come to terms with your dreams, it's even tougher to expect others to follow your dream path. As entrepreneurs, we have to choose. We have to make decisions, and sometimes they have to be split-second decisions. Sometimes, we're not able to do all of the analysis we'd like to make those decisions, but we still have to choose. Most of the time, deep down inside, we already know what to do. The hard part is actually doing it, because there's always comfort in taking the easy road. There's comfort in staying where you are, going with the majority, or listening to the naysayers and staying on their level. On the other hand, growth is often very painful, lonely, and inconvenient. When hardship and uncertainty come in life, we can't allow fear to keep us from making the tough decisions. Our lives depend on our ability to make those decisions.

At some point, you have to ask yourself: Are you content to merely exist, or will you choose to make that upward climb?

INNER MOUNTAIN JOURNAL

List the obstacles in your life that are keeping you from focusing on your goals and finishing. How can you change that?

_____

_____

_____

_____

_____

_____

_____

_____

DAY 5

WHEN YOU HAVE TO PUSH YOURSELF TO THE FINISH LINE: PRAYERFUL!

7

WHEN YOU HAVE TO GO IT ALONE

"Obstacles are distractions that can be defeated with desire and determination." ~Robert Shumake

BEFORE THE CLIMB:
MY DECISION TO RAISE MONEY FOR REPUBLICANS

RALPH WALDO EMERSON is quoted as saying, "Always do what you are afraid to do." That's a very powerful statement because in order to move forward to do what you are afraid to do, you have to first mentally psyche yourself up to do it. Most people are afraid of the hardships, the struggle, maybe even the rejection that they imagine they will experience if they begin living in a world they've never known before. I know because I entered such a world a decade ago, after I attended two fundraisers for the 2000 presidential election.

I went to a fundraiser for Vice President Al Gore and I felt like my little $2,000 was being taken for granted. Two weeks later, a friend I had met while attending Morehouse College invited me to an event for Texas Governor George W. Bush. I thought, *Bush? I don't know about that.* But I went—only because my friend had invited me. Sometimes, it's all about the relationships.

When I got there, Bush came up to me and gave me the "brother" handshake. The power of a handshake is a deep thing, showing that you know the code. Bush's handshake was not manufactured; it was real. It shocked me, so it piqued my interest. Afterwards, I spent 15 minutes talking to a guy by the name of Heinz Prechter about business. Prechter was a German immigrant who had made a fortune as the founder and CEO of the American Sunroof Company, a niche supplier to the automotive industry. I didn't know at the time that Prechter was also a major national fundraiser for the Republican Party, but I realized that he understood the intersection of business and politics. I recognized immediately that this guy had the kind of information and insight I was looking for. As we connected in conversation, I said to myself, *I don't know what this is, but I'm going to do it. I'm going to raise money for the Bush campaign.*

I went back to my friends and said, "Guys, I don't know where this is going to take me, but I'm going for it."

My best friend said to me, "Man, are you crazy? I can't be here. My mama would disown me. I can't even imagine that you're talking like this!" and he got up from the table and left. My best friend, who remains so to this day, crushed my heart with that move. Despite our difference of opinions, I went ahead with my fundraising plan anyway. I knew there was something there. I had to break through my fears. I was afraid. When your best friend tells you to beware of the course you're taking, you believe it a little bit. But he forced me into a gut-check moment that changed my life.

I didn't know what I was doing; I just called everybody. I would demand of people who knew me well, "Give me a hundred dollars!" My barber even gave me a check. I knew that most of the black community was resistant to republican candidates for president or any other office. But I told the people I contacted that politics is all about business. I told them all, "This is about dollars and cents. You need to take a closer look. This is not about the Republican or Democratic Party; this is about the Green Party—and I'm not talking about Ralph Nader. This is about business." That's how I laid it out.

I told them we needed people on both sides of the aisle. Malcolm X said it best: "When the white man tells you to go through door number one, and he goes through door number two, you need to follow him." Bush was going through a door that we weren't entering; yet, we wonder why all of us remain in a limited space in politics. When you see most of us in the process of politics, we're planning grass-roots efforts. We're always on the front line, the field director—the field hand, if you will. That takes you back to slavery times. I didn't want to be the field guy. No, I wanted to be where the finance was. I wanted to know where the money was.

What I learned was that you can fight racial prejudice—whether white prejudice or black prejudice—with superior knowledge, a command of the facts. One interesting encounter took place right after the 2004 election had ended. As one of the top fundraisers in the nation, I was invited to the Reynolds plantation in Georgia. I was one of three blacks at a lavish reception full of good food, drinks, and powerful, well-connected people. Most of the guests I met were not shy about asking me bluntly—and sometimes indignantly—"How did you get here?"

"Well, how did *you* get here?" I shot back. "I'm being rewarded for raising money. There is no affirmative action program for political fundraisers." But despite a few bumps and bruises along the way, I enjoyed my introduction to the world of political influence. This was a world where things happened quickly, where casual conversations led to multi-million-dollar deals. I was learning first-hand that being in the right place at the right time can make a difference that is not only strategic but life changing as well.

Climbing Kilimanjaro

DATE:
January 6, 2011

CAMPSITE:
Mweka (the descent site)

TEMPERATURE:
-15°/10°

ALTITUDE:
10,204 ft. above sea level

"Believe in Yourself as I believe in You": A Message from The Wiz

DAY FIVE QUICKLY turned into day six as Peter and I made our way toward my final destination. It was cold. I was tired, freezing and wheezing, but I never took my eye off the prize. I was way too motivated to stop now, but as usual, when things start going well in life, that's when the devil shows up to test and distract you.

We had been climbing for more than three hours when Peter started trying to convince me to go back. "It's too cold," he said, "You can't make it."

Truthfully, I partially believed him because he was my guide, but then again, all I wanted to do was see the sun come up. At that point, I really had to look inside myself to remember how I was trained and how I was brought up. Greater was He that was in me than he who was standing there telling me what I couldn't do. I remembered that I could do all things through Christ who strengthens me. All of a sudden, I was unfazed by his statement, and I told him to let me climb one more hour and we would be fine. I felt like Rocky Balboa, hyping myself up without any energy.

After that hour had passed, he came back to me and said, "The hour has gone by. We have to go back."

"Let me see if I can do one more hour," I said.

"But you're moving too slow."

I was really starting to get aggravated; so I asked him, "Is there an Olympic record for climbing a mountain? I'm not trying to break a record. I just want to go as far as I think I can go." We continued to go back and forth until finally, I told him that I just wanted to watch the sun come up.

He said, "The sunrise is going to take more time. You've been climbing all this time, climbing all these hours. I'm your guide, and you need to listen to me!"

Now I was angry. "If you're my guide, you need to be in front of me, but I'm in front of you! How am I in front of you?"

I couldn't believe that I was standing out there on a mountain in the freezing cold, arguing with the very person I had paid to see to it that I made it to my destination. Gone was the chilling bite of the icy 10-degree weather. Now, my blood was beginning to boil.

"You're supposed to listen to me; I'm your guide! You need to think about your children! You have three beautiful children at home to look after! You're going to die on this mountain!"

That did it. I had been climbing all night into what was now the next day. My chest was burning, my fingers and toes were frostbitten, and now this man had the nerve to speak about my children and tell me that I was going to die on this mountain after all I had gone through to get to this point? I lost it.

"Don't you talk about my kids," I spat. "I did not authorize you to speak to me about my children! You don't know them or me!"

He continued to argue with me, and all I wanted to do was climb until the sun came up. I felt in my spirit that if I could see the sun come up, then I would be able to go the distance. We climbed a few more hours, and then I began to see a hint of the sun on the horizon, peeking through the darkness. No sooner was I able to revel in my small victory then my guide was back in my face, telling me that we needed to go back. By this time, we had been climbing for eight to ten hours, but we were almost there ... at least I thought we were. I couldn't understand why the very person who should have been encouraging me the most was giving me such a hard time.

"We must go back," he said again, and then he grabbed me and pushed me. "You must listen to me!"

Now, I was livid. I told him, in no uncertain terms, that if he didn't take his hands off me, I was going to hurt him. My first thought was to hit him and fight him right there on the mountain, but I knew that if I would have done that, it would have taken me off my focus. When I thought about it later,

I was reminded of the scene when the devil tempted Jesus on the mountain. This was just another way for the enemy to try to keep me from focusing on achieving my goal, but I would not be discouraged. Yet, at that moment, I truly felt alone. Tib had reached the peak without me and had returned to report that it was a horrible experience. Now, I was facing my own nightmare, with my guide doing his best to turn me in the opposite direction.

Inner Mountain Introspective:
What Happens When You Have to Go at It Alone?

TIB AND I had been friends for 15 years. After he'd agreed to go with me, we'd planned our trip together and we'd trained together, but when I got sick, we agreed that if I wasn't strong enough, he would go on alone. And as it turned out, we both had to go on alone. That led me to wonder, *What happens when you have to go at it alone?* When people leave you, do you give up? When your business partners quit, do you stop writing your business plan? No!

Many of us long for someone that we can share our experiences with: an old friend, a relative, a college roommate. I wanted to have someone to endure the climb with, someone to cheer me on and tell me that I could do it. Many times in life, we think that when we start out with our friends, they're supposed to be our business partners, when in actuality, they shouldn't. When people fall off, we never consider the fact that maybe it's a gift that God has given us, or that maybe it's a plan or a special message that we have to continue to move forward on our own. Sometimes, you have to dig deeper and ask yourself, "Am I a trailblazer or am I a pathfinder?" In other words, what's your motivation? What is it that makes you eager to get out of the bed every morning and do whatever it is you do? What's your carrot, or purpose, in life? Both the hawk and the vulture are birds of prey, yet they operate in very different ways. The hawk, proud and majestic, is quick, calculating, and fierce in the hunt, while the vulture, bald and looming, sits back and waits patiently for the hawk to have his fill. When he is done, the vulture will happily feast on the leftovers.

The hawk is what we would call a trailblazer: he creates his own path. The vulture, however, is a pathfinder who uses a path that has already been forged by another and figures out how to use it to his advantage. At first glance, it would appear that the hawk would be the ideal choice because, let's face it, who wants to be known as a scavenger? But if you take a closer look, you will see that both birds are very well versed in keeping their stomachs full; one just works a little differently than the other.

Another example of the trailblazer and pathfinder dynamic would be the legacies of Bill Gates and Steve Jobs. Bill Gates, a trailblazer, created the operating system that runs our computers and co-founded Microsoft, the largest computer software company in the world. Steve Jobs, a pathfinder, was able to utilize the software ideas created by Gates, expound upon them, and then go on to create a series of revolutionary computer products (the iPod, iPhone, iPad, etc.) that have changed the course of technology. Though they chose different paths, both men accumulated great wealth as a result of their business choices and are legendary in their own rights. Can you imagine how different their stories may have been had they not focused on climbing their own personal mountains?

Looking back on that situation with Tib and me, I realized that I was put into a position where I was forced to be a trailblazer because I could not follow my guide's path. Had I done that, I probably would not have continued to climb. It's funny how God deals with people in different ways at different stages of their lives. Here I was, expecting Tib to come back from his journey with his usual words of encouragement, but it was just the opposite. He had nothing good to say about his experience, and his negative reaction immediately caused me to draw my own negative conclusions about something that I hadn't even experienced yet.

As entrepreneurs, we have to realize that we can't be brand new to ourselves. Half the time, when you are faced with an obstacle, you beat that obstacle. We have to stop comparing ourselves to others and compare ourselves to the greater good that we have. Picture yourself training for a marathon your entire life, and then the time to run the race finally arrives.

When the race begins, we are together at the starting line, and when you reach the five-mile line, you look around and find that you're still surrounded by 100 percent of the people with which you started. Then you approach the 15-mile mark, and find yourself with only 60 percent of the people with whom you started. At the 20-mile mark, you're all alone, still running toward the finish line, and then, with only 6.2 miles to go, somebody shows up on your path out of the bushes to complete the journey with you. Don't stop because the people that started with you don't end up with you, because they may be on a slower path. People with like minds and like visions will come out of the bushes to join you and help you along to see you to the finish line.

When going for greatness, you may end up alone when your friends say you can't or when the banks say it doesn't make sense. The question then becomes: Do you give up or go forward?

INNER MOUNTAIN JOURNAL

List something that you have been putting off because you were afraid to do it alone:

_____

_____

_____

_____

_____

_____

_____

_____

_____

8

THE RIGHT GUIDE CAN TAKE YOU TO THE SUMMIT

"Success always stands on the shoulders of giants. Whose shoulders are you standing on?" ~Robert Shumake

BEFORE THE CLIMB:
WHAT I LEARNED FROM MY WEALTHY MENTOR

WHEN I MET Heinz Prechter at the Bush fundraiser in 2000, I said to myself, *Whoever this guy is, he's a billionaire. I can learn something from him.* I wanted to know what kind of business he was in, how he operated, how he handled the interface of business and politics, which is what made him a household name in many circles—that, and the way he popularized the sunroof in the auto industry. Heinz Prechter also owned a chain of Michigan newspapers and ran a real estate development company, which made him a perfect mentor for me.

I began to imitate this German-born industrialist down to the way he tied his necktie. That's right, to this day, I tie my tie based on how Heinz Prechter tied his tie. I changed my tie from a half Windsor to a full Windsor. Even now, I never walk out of my house without a full Windsor tie around my neck. That was the power of imaging in the relationship we had developed. I'd decided that everything my new role model did, I was going to do. *He said he was a fundraiser? Well, I'm going to raise money*, I'd told myself. That's what I did.

I started interacting with the money guys. When I turned over the first $25,000 I'd raised for the campaign to Heinz, he was astonished. He said to me, "You raised that much money for me? You raised $25,000? How did you do it?"

I simply told him, "I raised a little bit from everybody I talked to, almost everybody I knew."

"You come with me. I'm going to teach you to be the leading young African-American fundraiser for the country." And he did. I went on to become one of the top fundraisers in the nation—black, white, or otherwise.

After that, I started flying around with him all over the country on his private plane. I was the youngest guy, by 12 to 15 years, of all the blacks who were working for the party in the country. I wasn't even 30 years old at the time. I learned about political fundraising from Heinz Prechter. More importantly, I was introduced to what it's like to rub elbows with the wealthiest, most accomplished, most powerful people in America. Heinz Prechter opened this door for me, but it wasn't like he gave me lessons. It was the power of influence. He told me, "If I could make just ten percent of all the money you're going to make, hanging out with me, *I* would be a rich man!" Of course, he already was a very rich man, but his point was well received.

Craig McCaw, the man who invented Nextel and then sold the company to Sprint for several billion dollars, the Vanderbilt family, still living on the wealth of their nineteenth-century ancestor, Cornelius Vanderbilt, who was a pioneer in shipping and railroads, super attorney Willie Gary, boxing impresario Don King—these were the people I began to meet over lunch and dinner. African-Americans like Gary and King were not in the majority; in fact, most of these high-level players were white men who had never had a face-to-face discussion with a black person. I needed to learn from them, but they also needed to learn from me. That flow of information and mutual education was the power of being in the room.

However, after a heady season of mentoring, a little more than one year after we'd met and our travels together began, Heinz Prechter ended his own life on July 6, 2001, during a tragic bout of depression. I was shocked and deeply saddened by the loss. He was only 59 years old, in his prime as a businessman and power broker. Fortunately, his legacy endures through the companies he founded and through the Heinz C. Prechter Bipolar Research Fund that his wife, Waltraud (Wally) Prechter, had established at the University of Michigan Health System, which is funding the medical study of the disease Heinz fought for much of his life. His life definitely endures in my mind and heart. I'm a different person because of what he showed and taught me.

New Guides Take Over—Just in Time

JUST AS I began to move forward and continue the climb by myself, I looked over and saw that Peter was vomiting off to the side. Then it hit me: he wanted to go back because he was sick and he was trying to psyche me out to make me think that I couldn't do it. He had tried to steal my dream from me! At that point, I had to look past my guide, and it was a real defining moment.

After I recognized that he was sick, I went to him and asked him to help me find another guide, and he met me with so much opposition! He told me that he would not help me find another guide because it would be "unprofessional." He just wouldn't do it.

"Fine," I shot back, "I don't need a guide; I'll just go by myself."

Now, I will admit that I was delirious. They say that God looks out for babies and fools, and for that, I am glad, because

I acted foolishly, and the very next step I took, I literally rolled down a cliff and bumped my head and tore my pants. My guide was convinced at that point. "Oh, my God," he said. "I will help you." And he did—he helped me find a new guide.

After a while, another guide approached us, and the two men spoke in Swahili for a few minutes. When their conversation ended, I was informed that the new guide had agreed to take me the rest of the way. I was happy that I had gotten through yet another obstacle in my climb, and now, I was ready to go with my new guide. As we started climbing, he encouraged me to take five steps and then breathe, so that's what I did.

After a couple of hours of climbing with my new guide, I asked him, "What is your name?" and amazingly enough, he told me that his name was Winnerson. I couldn't believe it. God had sent me a winner! That was a sign if I'd ever seen one. It's not every day that a "winner" comes to help you climb a mountain. That lit a fire of invigoration in my spirit.

"Tell Black America that we are one," he told me. "I'm going to take you to the mountaintop, my brother. I'm going to take you to the top for all black people."

Now, I had two things going on in my mind: On one hand, I was thinking, *Man, I ain't climbing for all black people, I don't even know them.* The other part of me was thinking, *Wow, this is a powerful experience, and I have a winner who is willing to embrace me and take me to the top of Mt. Kilimanjaro.*

By the time I had reached the summit, Ben, Tib's guide, had heard about what had happened with Peter and me, and he came up there to help me. He and Winnerson literally took me hand by hand and coached me by constantly telling me, "You can do it," and "You can make it," and "You're climbing for all black people."

"Forget that you were sick the other day," they told me. "Forget that you have asthma. You got this."

So I continued on to the top. I couldn't believe it. I had finally made it!

"I made it! I made it!" I yelled excitedly. "I made it to the top! Yeah, boy!"

"Well ... not really," Winnerson said, immediately killing my joy.

"What?" I responded, looking for signs that he was joking. As it turned out, we were only at the summit, which was technically the top of the mountain, but it wasn't the peak. If I wanted to go all the way, I would have to continue on to Uhuru Peak.

Uhuru Peak, which means "freedom" in Swahili, was another hour away, and I had nothing left. I was dead, and to make matters worse, there was no oxygen on the peak. So what do you do when you've got nothing left? You call upon the greatness inside you. You get with your prayer team, your squad, and you pull from your heart words of encouragement that confirm for you that you can do it. That was what Winnerson and Ben did for me.

To this day, I still don't know what they saw in me, but sometimes, other people see things in you that you don't see in yourself.

THE FINAL ASCENT: IT TAKES BRICK TO BEAT BRICK

THE EXPERIENCE OF making it to the summit made me realize just how vulnerable I really was in the grand scheme of things. My body was feeling every part of the mountain, and I still had a long way to go, but I knew I had to be tough, because when times get tough, you've got to get tough. It takes brick to beat brick. How do you cut through steel? With steel. Iron sharpens iron. Are you waiting for an opportunity? What things are you doing to prepare yourself for when opportunity shows up? What are you doing to sharpen your skills?

My toes where cracking against stone. My fingers felt as if

they were going to fall off at the joints. I had fallen down and I couldn't breathe, but still, I kept on climbing; even though so many obstacles had shown up to tell me, "You can't do this!" The Creator had already told me that I could.

When I started climbing with Winnerson, he told me to just take five steps and then breathe. Every time I'd look up at the top of the mountain in my fatigued condition, all I could think about was how massive it was, but I knew that if I could just focus on my feet and keep taking small steps, I would definitely get there. For me, there was power in mastering those small, detailed steps so I could get to the top.

Almost always in life when we are faced with a major goal or working on a big deal, fear just shows up and tries to derail us. Being a brick doesn't mean that you are a master of overcoming all of your obstacles in one fell swoop. It merely means that you have the wherewithal and mental fortitude to endure the process. So many times, we try to master the whole task, but if we learn to just master those small things, we can get there. After all, football games are won by feet, not yards. The 100-meter dash is won by tenths of seconds, and the long jump is won by inches.

Grinding out the drudgery of taking small steps, breathing, and doing it again paid off. The moment had arrived when I had no need to lift my weight upward or take another step forward. I had reached the peak of Mt. Kilimanjaro! After 12 hours, I had finally made it. When I'd started out, I had this idea that I was going to jump up and down when I finally made it to the top, but at that moment, I simply didn't have the energy, so I just kind of moved my arms around a little with the last bit of strength that I could muster, and I did one of those muscle man poses.

Even though I couldn't jump or leap, I was having an internal "I did it" party that could rival New Year's Eve in Times Square. I really don't remember the details of the six-hour descent back down the mountain to the campsite, but I knew that I had climbed for 18 hours that day and I had made it to the top, and that was all that mattered. I had come to climb Kilimanjaro—and that's exactly what I did.

INNER MOUNTAIN INTROSPECTIVE: WHAT HAPPENS WHEN YOU OUTGROW YOUR MENTOR?

IN LIFE, IT'S natural for us to want to find as many mentors as we can to give us advice and inspiration, but there comes a time when we outgrow our mentors and the student becomes the master. This occurs once the eagle has taught the eaglet that it can fly on its own.

My first guide had boasted about how he had climbed the mountain 150 times, and I was thrilled to have such an experienced guide who knew the lay of the land. But then he got sick. And not only did he get sick, he tried to steal my dream because his pride was so strong that, rather than admit that he was sick to save himself the embarrassment of allowing someone else to step in, he actually fought me on the mountain. In spite of that, I knew that I still had to accomplish my goal.

When we have a purpose in life, our advisors can only take us so far. In the end, we have to push past all to accomplish it. In *Star Wars*, Obi-Wan Kenobi taught Luke Skywalker all he could, but at some point, it was up to Luke to learn the practical application.

If your mentor is a real mentor, he or she will cheer you on. But your mentor will also recognize that you have to go where no man has gone before, so to speak. A depressor tries to steal your dreams. A detractor tells you what you're trying to accomplish is impossible. But a mentor, like a coach, gives you guidance and his or her objective is to see you win. For instance, although a coach might not ever have been an

Olympian or a champion of any kind, he takes great pride in seeing his athletes run faster or throw the ball further than he ever could. Your mentor will give you the insight or the lesson, but we always have to go at it alone at the end of the day.

When you recognize that you've reached a point as a student when you have moved beyond your guide, remember that the only guide who will always be with you is the Creator. If you are willing to keep moving, God will bring you a winner to help you complete your journey in spite of the naysayers, and winners know how to get there because they've been there before!

INNER MOUNTAIN JOURNAL

WHO ARE YOUR MENTORS? WHAT HAVE THEY TAUGHT YOU?

_____

_____

_____

_____

_____

_____

_____

_____

_____

_____

Day 6

THE RIGHT GUIDE CAN TAKE YOU TO THE SUMMIT: I MADE IT TO THE TOP OF THE MOUNTAIN AT UHURU!

GIVING GLORY TO GOD!

AT THE PEAK OF MT. KILIMANJARO

9

HANDLE VICTORY WITH GRACE

"Train the mind; the body will follow." ~Robert Shumake

BEFORE THE CLIMB:
LESSONS FROM TRACK AND FIELD

TRACK AND FIELD helped to shape me into the person I am today. It taught me how to win—even if victory cost me all I had. It taught me how to use my gifts to get back on top—even if I fell all the way to the bottom. Track also taught me how to stay focused enough to keep winning, how to stay on top after I reach my goals.

My start in track and field seemed to be nothing more than a fluke, an emotional response to a dare that had put my health at risk. Growing up asthmatic, kids would tease me all the time. Of course, I didn't like that. Once, one of them predicted, "We're going to race, and you're going to go to the hospital." He laughed. So we had a race to the first fire hydrant . . . and afterward, I immediately went to the hospital.

When I returned, the same kid said, "Yeah, you beat me, but you went to the hospital. Let's race further, and I'll beat you this time." So instead of racing to the first fire hydrant, we raced to the next fire hydrant. I beat him again, but they had to take me to the hospital again. The taunting continued, so we raced a third time, this time, to the end of the block. I beat him and kept running, past the end of the block. Somehow, I ran past the point of an asthma attack, past what I thought was my limit. I've been running ever since. Beating my opponent and beating asthma on my block had convinced me that I could compete in track and field. That small victory taught me to constantly do little things to push myself past my limits, increase my endurance, and enlarge my capacity to succeed.

I became a long-jumper, hurdler, and relay guy for my high school team at Detroit Denby. We had a super-fast team. Runners on my team went to the Olympic Trials. We were the state champs in every event from the 100-meter dash to the 800-meter run. I wasn't the fastest guy on the team, but I worked the hardest. Going into the state championship meet during my senior year, I had the fastest time in the state of Michigan in the 330-yard low hurdles. The 330 lows was a tough-man's race. I also had the state's best record in the long jump. I was the city champ, the conference champ, and the favorite for those two events going into the state championships. But I attended my prom the night before and got food poisoning. I bombed out on the day of the state meet. No college scholarship for me. It was literally the worst day of my life. I suddenly found myself unable to go to school, still living in my family's raggedy house. I was forced to take a job at Toys 'R' Us. I'd told myself that my life was over.

I began to party every day. I drank every day, something I had never done in high school. With no hope for the immediate future, my thought at the time was, "This is all I got." However, track and field once again came to my rescue. Six months into my job at Toys 'R' Us, a buddy of mine noticed in the newspaper that an indoor track meet was coming up soon, and he encouraged me to sign up and participate. At first, I blew it off, telling him and myself that I didn't have time, but then I reconsidered. *You know what,* I said to myself, *I'm gonna go see if I've still got it.*

I competed in the meet and ran my fastest time ever in the hurdles. I made my longest jump ever. I was literally jumping for my life. After I won the long jump, I sent a newspaper clipping about the meet to a college track coach I had met in high school. He looked at the results and asked me, "You jumped this far? You want to go to college? Can you be here in two weeks?" My answer was "Yes" to all three questions. That's how I'd gotten into college, with a full scholarship to Ferris State University in Big Rapids, Michigan. A few weeks later, I competed for Ferris State in the conference championship.

I learned in track and field to focus on the finish line, not on the guy to the right or the left of me. When you keep your eyes on that goal, that's what really matters in the end. Then, after you have beaten the competition, won the race, and can savor the victory, you have to maintain the posture (and the humility) of a true champion. You have to remember that *you* are your number one competitor and continue to challenge yourself. You have to keep pushing yourself because you are your benchmark—not the next person. In every contest, expect to be the leader and always expect to win.

VIEW FROM THE MOUNTAINTOP: TOTAL REFLECTION

WHEN I TOOK the final steps that lifted me to the top of the mountain, I was exhausted, sore, and of course, oxygen deprived. Everything was blurry. I was seeing spider webs and animals that didn't exist at that altitude, such as buffaloes and bears. My three toes that were now missing toenails ached. My body was beaten up from the punishment of the weather on the mountain as well as the physical work I had done during the climb.

The vast view before me at the top of Mount Kilimanjaro was breathtaking. I could see Kenya, not just Tanzania. I understood, in a new way, the power of visualization. I saw what Dr. King saw when he made his "I've Been to the Mountaintop" speech on the last night of his life. I saw what Moses saw when he ascended to the top of Mount Horeb to receive the Ten Commandments from God. I saw what Jesus saw when he would go to the mountains to pray, and at one point, experienced a transfiguration.

We all have our mountaintop moments, whether we're climbing a physical mountain or a spiritual mountain. We're all ordinary people, but some of us can do extraordinary things. We should treasure those moments at the top. My climb up Kilimanjaro put me in touch with how vulnerable I was as a human being, but also connected me with how powerful I was. Once I got to the top of the mountain, I forgot about the struggle. I had gone through sandstorms, deserts, rainstorms, and hailstorms to get there. But the storm always comes before the rainbow.

I was tired. I was sleepy. Because of the oxygen deprivation, because of the bitter cold, if I had stopped to rest for a lengthy period at the top of the mountain, I would have died. After a half hour at the mountain's peak, my guides told me, "We must go, Mr. Robert."

RETURN OF THE HERO

DAY SEVEN WAS very symbolic in many different ways. Not only was it the last day of my excursion, but the number seven is also the number of completion. Though I had experienced a lot over the previous six days, it wasn't over yet … I still had to descend the mountain.

It took four hours to get back down Kilimanjaro. I had to focus the entire time on putting right foot over left with my toenail-less foot banging on rocky terrain the whole way down. When I reached the bottom, I immediately gave away all the gear I had purchased to the people who had helped me climb—jacket, shoes, socks, everything. Not only was I grateful to them for helping me achieve my goal, but I never wanted to think about doing that ever again.

The people in the village cheered for me and told me that I was like Iron Man and Superman. "You're a man among men," they told me because they didn't think that I would make it. "The Black American was sick," they said, "but he did it! He did it for all black people." I was ecstatic.

During the two-hour ride back to the hotel, I popped open a bottle of Cristal that I had waiting for me to celebrate the occasion. I had done it! I had accomplished what nobody thought I could do, asthma and all.

When I finally arrived at the hotel, all I could think about was taking a nice, relaxing hot shower and getting some rest. As I started to undress, a horrible odor filled the room, and it actually took a few seconds for me to realize that it was coming from me. It had been seven days since my last shower, and I smelled awful. That was another humbling experience for me because I could identify with how homeless people must feel, and why they sometimes don't want to shower, as I've heard. My skin was so tender that I was afraid of the water hitting my body. The tiny beads of water felt like thousands of needles piercing my skin. It literally hurt to get clean.

When I finally reflected on everything I had experienced over the previous seven days, I reveled in the fact that I had overcome it all and climbed to the top of Mt. Kilimanjaro. I had seen and experienced beauty beyond measure, my body had been broken and bruised, I had died to my physical restraints and overcome my greatest fear—my asthma. I had talked with God and His angels, and I had endured frostbite and immense pain.

I felt like Moses on the mountaintop, still in awe after having had his conversation with God. Most importantly, I had been transformed and had grown as a man.

INNER MOUNTAIN INTROSPECTIVE:
NEVER ALLOW ANYONE TO STEAL YOUR DREAM

THERE ARE MANY friends and associates who are best described as dream stealers. These are people who try to tell you that you should be doing something different with your life because they can't see your vision. It's okay that they can't, because it's your vision and you're the only one who needs to see it. After all, God gave it to you.

When Peter tried to make me go back, I was infuriated because I felt like he was trying to rob me. Instead of just dealing with the fact that he was sick, he tried to steal my dream by making me think that I wasn't strong enough to make it. He began to play mind games with me to take my focus off of what I was there to do. He even offered to give me the certificate, certifying that I had made it to the top, and he promised not to tell anyone if only I would go back, but I refused to give in because I wanted it that badly. I couldn't allow myself to take that piece of paper, knowing very well that I hadn't done the work. I would have lost so much more had I allowed him to convince me to turn my back on everything I believed in to take the easy way out.

The Creator has given everyone the right to prosper, but it's up to you to decide whether you are up for the challenge. Dream chasing isn't easy, and it is not for the faint of heart. Physical strength has nothing to do with passion or drive. Once you have made up your mind to do something, you have to be willing to get right down to where the rubber meets the road and put in the work.

If asked where the wealthiest place in the world is, most people would probably say Fort Knox or the U.S. Treasury, right? Wrong! The wealthiest place in the world is the graveyard. The graveyard is where countless people have taken their billion-dollar dreams and ideas with them, never to be discovered.

People know to ask a mechanic about their cars, but when it comes to making money, we seem to always ask people who don't have any. You should never ask a person who makes $30,000 how to make $100,000. If they've never done it before, how can you logically expect them to show you how to do it? Dream stealers come a dime a dozen. They may be disguised as friends, or they may even be family members, but you cannot allow them to deter you. Often, people only know what they know and don't have the ability to see past their current situations, so they're not equipped to support what they don't understand; and sometimes, your so-called friends are content with their own mediocrity and just don't want to see you surpass them in life. While you still love your friends and family, achieving your goals may require you to love them at arm's length if they are preventing you from moving forward. Never forget that the "I'm Gonna" and the "Never Say Die" Tribes cannot co-exist on the same reservation.

In order to be successful, you have to surround yourself with positive people who appreciate your passion, understand your goals, and can help you get to where you want to be. Never forget that you were created in the image of God, and He says in His Word that you are more than a conqueror, and that He that is in you is stronger than he that is in the world. That lets you know that you are already divinely equipped with everything you need to be successful in life. The question is: are you ready to tap into it? If you are, then you are well on your way to tackling the task of climbing your Inner Mountain. The task won't be easy, but once you've made it to the top, your life will never be the same.

INNER MOUNTAIN JOURNAL

LIST A TIME WHEN YOU HAVE ACCOMPLISHED A GOAL THAT
SEEMED IMPOSSIBLE. WHAT IS YOUR NEXT "IMPOSSIBLE" GOAL?

_____

_____

_____

_____

_____

_____

_____

_____

_____

10

BEYOND THE MOUNTAINTOP

<hr>

"It's the repetition of affirmations that leads to belief. And once that belief becomes a deep conviction, things begin to happen."
~Muhammad Ali

BEFORE THE CLIMB:
PLANTING SEEDS THAT BEAR FRUIT

I BEGAN THIS book telling you how Steve Myen inspired me to climb Mt. Kilimanjaro. I briefly described his success in the commercial real estate business and how he become a great advisor and mentor to me, and above all, how he grew to be one of my closest friends. I continue to reflect on the many ways Steve was always there as an ally, as a resource, as a quiet cheerleader. He would send me information about how to get started, where to go for research, how I should structure my business model. The boost Steve gave me was like the water, fertilizer, and sunshine that turn a seed into a sapling and then a great tree that bears ripe, delicious fruit.

When I was a boy, my grandmother used to have my siblings and me lay the seeds from apples and oranges in the sunlight on her windowsill to dry out. "We are going to plant these seeds so that orchards can grow," she told us, and she explained why it was important for us to leave something behind for the next generation. Even as a child, my grandmother's statement had a huge impact on me. Her words returned to me one day when

I was shopping for some watermelon and oranges, and the grocer asked me, "Seed or seedless?" As I stood there weighing my options, it occurred to me that with all of our urgency, and the get-it-quick mentality, we weren't setting ourselves up to leave anything to the next generation. My determination is to build my businesses to the point where I can continually invest in institutions and programs that help young people reach their destinations. I challenge myself on a daily basis to push myself, to continue to improve. That's one of the secrets of success.

The climb up Kilimanjaro really did transform my life. It reminded me that my life has value. Every day during the climb, I was thinking about what I had missed, mistakes I had made. I wanted to take those experiences on the mountain and use them in my life. The climb compelled me to come back and reinvent. As a result, I was a greater, more focused man after climbing that mountain. After that, it never was about the business alone. I was determined to make a difference in my life first and make money second. I emerged as a greater businessman than I'd ever been before.

Standing at the top of Uhuru Peak in the first month of 2011, I recognized that I needed to be free. Although I'd built a business and made millions of dollars, I really had not experienced true freedom. Freedom to me meant making a significant difference. I imagined that what I was seeing and feeling at the peak of Kilimanjaro was akin to the kind of experience that Dr. King had tried to explain to his last audience when he told them he had been to the mountaintop and seen the Promised Land. What I saw from Uhuru Peak was the promise of freedom.

As I savored that moment—as cold and exhausted as I was—I asked myself what I would do if I could redraft my life right then and there. I realized that I had to be honest about how I felt operating in my hometown. I didn't want to be there fulltime. I enjoyed traveling. I enjoyed seeing the world. I enjoyed the smiles I could put on children's faces in Ghana, in Ethiopia, in the Dominican Republic, and Haiti. That, to me, was real freedom. I needed to put myself in a position to contribute and do those things. If I made money, then great. If I didn't, it didn't matter; so I knew that whatever I touched needed to be international. I realized that I held my own destiny. I had climbed a mountain in a foreign land, and I realized that I had to be global.

I also realized that character is what really matters. Character is the tree. Reputation is the branches. Reputation changes like the wind. Character defines who you are. I decided I wanted to be like the Jewish community, which finds perpetual motivation in the words "never again." Never again should I put myself in a position where I'm tied to any market condition, tied to any political regime. I needed to be free to do the thing I wanted to do, serve humanity. I really am a humanitarian. I'm a social entrepreneur by nature. I had already given 100 college scholarships to students. In 2008, I had started the HBCU Cross Country Championships to celebrate athletes at historically black colleges and universities who run long distance races in parks, golf courses, and the woods each fall. I recognized that I wanted to be involved in ventures like that all the time. Being bound in those years of litigation and bitter fights kept me from doing what I really was called here to do, and that is to serve people. I'm gifted to be a great businessman, and that can help lots of folks out of poverty. I've had the Midas touch, but after the wars I had been through, my hands were sore.

HONORARY CONSUL GENERAL: "YOUR EXCELLENCY"

AS I CONTINUED to visualize myself as a man walking in international favor and flair, all of a sudden, what I imagined started to take form in ways I had never expected. Thanks to the contacts I had made in Africa before, during, and after my Kilimanjaro climb, I became an honorary consul general for two countries: Botswana, the number one exporter of diamonds in the world, and Tanzania, home to the continent's highest peak. I began representing Botswana in May 2012 and Tanzania in June 2012. My appointment as honorary consul general of Trinidad and Tobago came later, in May 2013. For the most part, I promote trade and investment in those nations in the United States, but I can represent them anywhere in the world.

It's really amazing to realize that my new international life began with a simple desire, then expanded into what I believed international life should look like for me. Being a diplomat means two countries have come together to embrace you. The country you want to represent goes through its background checks, and then the U.S. has to decide whether to accept you as a diplomat. Now that I have crossed that threshold, I can sit down and give international leaders and fellow diplomats advice on business, financial, political, and social issues. It really is amazing to be a diplomat in a foreign country and to be referred to as "Your Excellency." I get regular calls from government ministers and even heads of state. I have made so many friends in countries beyond the U.S. And it all began with the international perspective inspired by my Kilimanjaro climb.

I recently had the opportunity to tour a diamond mine. I saw the DeBeers diamond-making process and held a 300-carat diamond in my hand. Recognizing the amount of heat and pressure that diamond had to go through to come out as the world's most coveted gemstone, I realized that we are no different. But instead of diamond mines, we should focus on our diamond *minds*. With the wisdom and fortitude forged by my mountain-climbing experience, anything is possible. Stay tuned.

See you at the next mountain.

Inner Mountain Introspective: What's Your Motivation?

WHEN YOU FOCUS on climbing your Inner Mountain, it forces you to look within and ask yourself what kind of person you are. Are you a trailblazer or a pathfinder? A hawk or a vulture? When determining how we will conquer our individual mountains, we must determine our paths and take responsibility for our successes as well as our failures. When I started the business, initially, it was about making money, but I learned very quickly that "making it" as a motivation didn't last. I had to have something else that moved me. Was it my kids' college educations, the number of scholarships I could create, buying my first home? What? Why am I here?

My motivation on the mountain became seeing Brother John's bright, encouraging smile every morning when he woke me up and then hearing the Masai men sing at the end of each day. Their chants touched my soul. They sang songs of Hallelujah in Swahili and they sang with the spirit of angels. This ritual became my inspiration.

After the first day, I was tearful. It was touching to hear people sing to motivate me, and I will always love and have affection for the continent where I heard the Masai Warriors sing. It made me feel like I was going through my own rite of passage.

After I survived my asthma attack, my motivation became proving to myself, the Masai Warriors, my guide, and everyone else in the world who'd said I couldn't do it that I was stronger than my circumstances. That was my carrot. When striving for your goals and dreams, you've got to have a reason for life. Once you've made your first million, it's not about the money anymore. At that point, it becomes more about keeping score; it's the game!

As you climb your Inner Mountain, are you willing to break yourself and recreate yourself? Many times, you can sit around and talk about what you want to do in a great business, but before long, you let your dream and your plans go. But there comes a time when you have to go at it alone. In climbing your Inner Mountain, we all have to go with our internal fortitude. It's not physical. It's internal. We really can climb mountains. We can create mountains because we say so. The mountains host obstacles we perceive because we take our eyes off the goal.

Our successes and failures are all based on our thoughts and actions. If we focus on that, anything is possible.

WHAT IT WAS LIKE

BY: TEBEBU TSADIK

"Even though we started out on the journey together, it turned out that we were not destined to end it that way." ~Tebebu Tsadik

HAD I KNOWN what I was getting into when Robert Shumake invited me to climb Mt. Kilimanjaro with him, I probably would have respectfully declined while running full speed in the opposite direction. Part of the reason was that I had no mountain-climbing experience, but as fate would have it, I took the opportunity to take the journey of a lifetime with a man for whom I have grown to have a tremendous amount of respect.

Though we have known each other for many years, our trip to Africa showed me a completely different side of my friend. The first day we started the hike, our hearts were filled with laughter, singing, and camaraderie. We were excited about the prospect of making it to the top of that majestic mountain, but little did we know how much our wills would be tested along the way.

The hike started at Machame Gate at an altitude of just over 1700m. The start of the walk was through a humid rainforest and was quite gentle overall. Surrounded by the warm and welcoming African climate that greeted us with an 80-degree temperature, this part of the hike was easy. As we got higher, the air and vegetation thinned out, yet the views were spectacular. At night, we camped in tents and watched the sunset from the side of the mountain. It was remarkable.

On the first night, we camped at Machame and the second night at Shira Plateau. From the height of 3700m, we were clearly above the clouds and sometimes waves of fog would take over the entire mountain. On the third day, our "altitude acclimatization" day, we ascended to over 4500m at the Lava Tower before dropping back down to camp at Barranco Hut below 3900m.

Each camp was different but equally beautiful. This was the morning that Robert woke me up, gasping for air to breathe. It was probably the pivotal point of the trip (in my opinion) and the test of Robert's mental strength. To stay alive, he had to take not one but two tanks of oxygen and descend immediately. However, he refused to give up and decided to continue upward. I remember wondering while we were walking together how I was going to make it. For a while, I started to question my objective, doing it alone did not make sense. But then again, I felt that there was no reason for both of us not to make it. After all, we had flown all the way from the USA to Tanzania to get to the top of Mt. Kilimanjaro. Therefore, I kept on trekking upward.

Then there he was, beside me, taking his vitamins and doing his inhaler. I watched him struggle, and some of the steps that he took were baby steps, but he stayed strong. I was impressed by the determination and strength of Robert Shumake and concluded that he would make it to the top.

Even though we started out on the journey together, it turned out that we were not destined to end it that way. Circumstances beyond our control dictated the need for each of us to go to the top alone. Though we did not understand it at the time, looking back on it now, I understand that God has a purpose for everything.

On day four, I trekked from Karanga Valley to the Barafu Camp with relatively little effort. When I arrived, I was feeling good and full of energy. After a conversation with my guide, Ben, I opted to continue to Uhuru Peak the same day instead of spending the night at Barafu Camp. Looking back, it was the biggest mistake as well as the best decision I'd made.

On one hand, it was a mistake because it took everything out of me, almost to the point of giving up on my journey to the top. On the other hand, I am glad I opted to go forward because this part of the expedition tested my willpower and by far was one of the biggest challenges that I have experienced in my life.

The trek to the peak was a major shock. I had to stop regularly to let my legs recover. My legs were tired, and each step took much concentration and effort. Climbing Mount Kilimanjaro means progressing through a succession of distinct climates and weather. I experienced every conceivable weather condition, from the howling windstorms, to the dense and impenetrable fog, to blistering sun, unfathomable snow, and rain, within a matter of minutes. While going through these courses, you learn to appreciate the work of the Creator and his power.

At the end of this immense challenge, the reward was breathtaking. Reaching the top of this massive place, the Uhuru peak (meaning "freedom" in Swahili), also known as "The Roof of Africa," was the most exhilarating experience. It was an amazing sight and the completion of an enormous effort.

As I stood on that massive expanse that is Mt. Kilimanjaro, it made me appreciate that in the grand scheme of things, where I saw myself alone, I was minuscule and powerless. I also learned that in a split second, my life could take a different turn. The rock I stood on could give in, the hiking boots I trusted could lose their footing, and I could be deprived of oxygen at any given time. In that instant, I learned humility and appreciated how precious life was. The seven-day experience became the experience of my lifetime.

On the way to the summit, as I clung to my life, wondering what I was doing in this no man's land, all I was thinking was, *I should be with my two boys, my wife, and my close family*, as if I might never see them again. The altitude made it difficult to take on oxygen, and the muscles in my legs felt weak. At one point, I told Ben I was so tired that I could not go on any further and that I needed to take a break. Ben always encouraged me to take as many breaks as I needed to ensure that I made it all the way. However, at this moment, I needed a little more than a break. As I leaned on a huge rock, I remember wanting to close my eyes and take a two or three minute catnap, which I thought was what I needed at the time. Ben, standing next to me, started shaking me, and with a daunting voice, he said, "No, you cannot close your eyes here! If you close your eyes, you will never wake up!"

Little did I know that I was beginning to feel the effect of the altitude. I was fatigued and started having a throbbing headache. I was having shortness of breath, persistent coughing, and I began to vomit. Vomiting was an immense and immediate relief.

I remember telling Robert after I came back from Uhuru Peak that it was a horrible experience as he was waiting to climb the next day. It sounded like a discouraging statement at the time, but that is exactly how I felt! By that time, I had trekked for more than 15 hours, my body ached all over, and I was bone tired. I was exhausted, both mentally and physically, and all I wanted to do was sleep. I had no physical or mental strength to explain anything.

Several hours later, I was glad to see Robert returning from the top. He arrived at the camp, supported by other guides from a different camp. His mountain gear was tattered, boots dilapidated, and his gloves shredded. His face was full of sand as if somebody had dragged him from the mountaintop, and these were all signs of his struggle and determination. I did not have to ask Robert how it was, because his appearance was full of answers.

Yet, of the two of us, I had been the fortunate one, because under the patient yet persistent coaching and encouragement of my guide, I climbed the mountain with only myself to battle. The irony to that was that when we departed on our way to the

CLIMBING YOUR INNER MOUNTAIN

top, we decided for Robert to hike with the senior guide and myself with his assistant.

Robert, on the other hand, was faced with many obstacles along the way. His health was challenged from the hiccups he'd had for five hours or so on day two, to the asthma attack on day three. At one point, it almost seemed as if the devil himself was trying to stop him. Peter, the senior guide, the very person who was supposed to take him to the top, was standing in his way. He had objected to going up the mountain because he did not believe that Robert had anything left in him to accomplish his mission. Plus, the guide himself had gotten an altitude sickness and ended up taking a tank of oxygen after he descended to where I was waiting for Robert. Nevertheless, by the grace of God, Robert emerged victorious.

Robert has such a strong personality, and he taught me a lot along the way. I watched him as he overcame hardship after hardship, and I appreciated his perseverance, determination, and willingness to go the extra mile, even when it was seemingly impossible. As the old saying goes, his attitude had determined his altitude. Having to witness what he went through, including not being able to breathe at 3900m above sea level, I can't help but to appreciate his determination.

Even though climbing Mt. Kilimanjaro was never on a to-do list in my life, I was very happy to be part of this voyage with Robert. Most importantly, I would not have wanted to do it with anyone else.

How To Climb Your Inner Mountain is much more than just a story about a man who climbed a mountain and lived to tell about it; it is a testament to how we can pull forth the things that lie buried deep inside of ourselves in order to overcome the mountains in our lives. From my personal experience of climbing the mountain, and from the perspective of watching my friend climb through adversity, I learned many valuable life lessons, and it is my hope that this story will contribute something of sincere value to yours as well.

Equipment List

PURCHASED FROM BACKCOUNTRY NORTH

www.backcountrytc.com

Essential Items

Duffel bag - Large enough for all climbing gear and clothing to be carried by the porters along with an extra bag to be left at the hotel with extra gear
Small luggage lock - to lock zippers
Day backpack - between 20 - 35 liters. Large enough to carry your water, camera, raincoat, lunch pack, snacks & warm clothing
Sleeping bag
Ski-pole / walking stick
Water bottle / containers
Kilimanjaro map (Can be bought at Park gate)

High Altitude Gear

Waterproof, breathable & windproof jacket
(outer wear like Ventex, Gore-Tex or Jeantex)
Waterproof, breathable & windproof pants
Polar fleece (middle layer)
Thermal underwear (under layers)
Mittens or warm gloves
Glove liners (if necessary)
One pair thermal (polertex) socks
Balaclava
Gaiters
Thermal water flask

Hiking Gear

Shorts
Hiking pants
Regular underwear
T-shirts
Raincoat or Poncho

FOOTWEAR

Water resistant semi-stiff hiking boots – mid-weight boots work great
Shoes for overnight camps - i.e. sneakers, running shoes, etc.
Socks - several pairs for the climb
Liner socks - to keep your feet dry and limit the risk of blisters

EQUIPMENT

Sun hat or similar (with a brim)
Collapsible ski stick (optional but highly recommended)
Water bottles - two or three (capacity at least 6 liters)
Head lamp, good strong one with spare batteries and an extra light bulb
Water purification tablets
Sunglasses- good quality dark lenses for the climb, with a securing strap
Flashlight (torch) with spare batteries

PERSONAL ITEMS

Toiletry kit (soap, toothbrush, wet wipes, etc.)
Towel
Sun screen and lip protection, SPF 30+
Ziploc bags to protect camera, etc. from dust
Toilet paper
Money belt for passport and valuables

MEDICAL AND FIRST AID SUPPLIES

Headaches - Syndols
Altitude sickness-Diamox (if not allergic to sulpha)
Diarrhea - Imodium
Nausea - Valoid
Malaria - Prophylaxis
Water purification tablets
Painkillers
Muscular sprains
Abrasions blisters and cuts - Plaster, bandages
Antiseptic cream - Betadine
Flu and colds
Eye drops
Insect repellent

OPTIONAL ITEMS

Camera, extra lenses and film (ASA 200 film recommended)
Binoculars
Powdered sports drinks for the climb (ex. Game or Isotonic drinks)
Pocket knife
Notebook & pencil
Plastic bags to keep clothing dry (masking tape)
Energy snacks and sweets
Video camera, tapes, battery packs, and tri-pod

LETTERS

Mr Robert
Thanks for Starting 2011 with you its amazing
trip with both of you
But im very Sorry and i apologize for what
happen the time we went the top on the way
I was got Sick and i fell to take you all the
way to uhuru IM REAL SORRY FOR THAT.
Please forgive and forget what happen.
Peter nathan

FROM PETER, MY FIRST GUIDE.

To

MR Robert.
It's nice time to say thanks
very much to take you to the peak
of Africa This was amazing day
because I like Americans especially
the $"BLACK ONE".
Please send much greetings to
All Blacks American Say's African
we are together
Your
Winnerson.

FROM WINNERSON, THE "WINNER" THAT GOD SENT ME.

FROM BENNY, THE ASSISTANT GUIDE WHO TOOK TIB TO THE PEAK.

Jan 07/11

Congratulations on making it to the top. Remember that 18 yr olds always know whats right! It was nice meeting you.

from your Canadian friend
Mariah Carey Zalitah.

FROM MARIAH CAREY ZALITAH, A YOUNG GIRL FROM THE VILLAGE WHO CHEERED FOR ME WHEN I RETURNED FROM CLIMBING KILIMANJARO.

CLIMBING YOUR INNER MOUNTAIN

Jan 07/2011

Ça a été très sympa de vous
rencontrer - or in english it was very
nice to meet you.
We all get to the top!

Fran Nagali (France)

FROM FRAN NAGALI, A WOMAN FROM FRANCE WHO CLIMBED IN MY
GROUP.

About the Author

ROBERT S. SHUMAKE, is a leading private equity investor and real estate developer. He has built a real estate portfolio of nearly three million square feet and financed over $1 billion. Shumake is the CEO of Shumake Global Partners, L3C, a provider of socially beneficial services in the areas of technology, real estate, education, agriculture, housing and infrastructure, energy, healthcare, and finance. He is an active supporter of youth, orchestrating fundraising events to ensure that they become and remain viable citizens. The Robert S. Shumake Scholarship Relays has supported over 10,000 student athletes. The Shumake Family and Friends Foundation has provided over 200 college scholarships since its inception in 2004. He founded the Shumake Legacy Academy to educate 3000 HIV-infected orphans in Addis Ababa, Ethiopia.

Robert Shumake holds an honorary doctorate from Lewis College of Business in Detroit. He is currently honorary consul to Botswana, Tanzania, and Trinidad and Tobago. Shumake's success is driven by his philosophy of life: "I always want to promote the double bottom line: make a profit in business and make a difference in the community."

To book Robert Shumake

for speaking engagements and book signings, please email
Trea Davenport at Trea Day Management & Publicity
TreaDayPR@gmail.com

Connect With Robert Shumake Online:

Website: www.RobertShumake.com

Company Website: www.RobertShumake.com

Shumake Relays: www.ShumakeRelays.com

Facebook: www.Facebook.com/RobertSShumake

Twitter: www.Twitter.com/RobertShumake